Microsco

MW01599209

Grades 5-8

Written by Kim & Scott Taylor, Wendy Gauthier, Brenda Chapman
Illustrated by Tom Riddolls

About the authors: Kim Taylor has been involved in teaching science and environmental studies to children in a variety of settings for 10 years. Kim's academic qualifications include Honours Bachelor of Science and Bachelor of Education degrees. She is an experienced science writer, creating teacher professional development resources in science for early years educators and elementary teachers.

Scott Taylor has been involved in teaching science and history to children in a variety of settings for 10 years. Scott's academic qualifications include a Master's degree in History and a Bachelor of Education degree. Scott is an experienced writer, having written a number of articles and educator professional development resources.

Wendy Gauthier, a computer specialist, has kept her students involved with new teaching strategies and incorporated them into her daily lessons and long term goals for 30 years. Wendy was the recipient of the Teacher of the Year Award from the Rainbow District School Board in 2006.

Brenda Chapman, as part of her 33-year-career, taught intermediate science by capitalizing on students' curiosity and love of experimenting for themselves. She is now retired and enjoying a new career in Fine Art.

ISBN 978-1-55035-777-1
Copyright 1993
Revised January 2007
All Rights Reserved * Printed in Canada

Published in the United States by:
On The Mark Press
3909 Witmer Road PMB 175
Niagara Falls, New York
14305
www.onthemarkpress.com

Published in Canada by:
S&S Learning Materials
15 Dairy Avenue
Napanee, Ontario
K7R 1M4
www.sslearning.com

At  Glance

Learning Expectations	Skills Acitvities	Physical Science	Human Science	Single-Celled Organisms	Animal Science	Plant Science
Language Skills						
• Reading comprehension	•	•	•	•	•	•
• Communicating in writing	•	•	•	•	•	•
• Vocabulary development	•	•	•	•	•	•
• Creating reports		•	•	•	•	•
Reasoning & Critical Thinking Skills						
• Generating questions		•	•	•	•	•
• Comparing and contrasting	•	•	•	•	•	•
• Developing research skills	•	•	•	•	•	•
• Observation and analysis	•	•	•	•	•	•
• Applying knowledge	•	•	•	•	•	•
• Self-evaluation		•	•	•	•	•
Physical Skills						
• Hand-eye coordination	•	•	•	•	•	•
• Measuring accurately	•	•	•	•	•	•
• Drawing diagrams	•	•	•	•	•	•
Understanding						
• How to use a microscope	•	•	•	•	•	•
• How to prepare different types of samples	•	•	•	•	•	•
• When to use different types of samples	•	•	•	•	•	•

Microscopy

Table of Contents

Microscopy

Microscopy

Introduction

The skill of observing could arguably be considered to be the most important science skill. An observation is an experience gained through the senses. Most often, this sense is the sense of sight, but observations can also be made using the senses of touch, hearing, taste and smell.

Observing does not simply mean looking at something. When observing we look closely and purposefully in order to gain greater understanding of objects and events in the world around us.

The human eye is a powerful observing device, but it has its limitations. The sense of sight can be extended using optical instruments which magnify objects and make their inner and outer details available to us. Instruments such as hand lenses, magnifying glasses, tripod-mounted lenses, dissecting and compound microscopes can all be used in the classroom to enable students to extend their sense of sight.

This book enables students to make observations using the eye, hand lenses and compound microscopes. The focus is, however, on the compound microscope. Students will learn important skills for observing, recording observations, and manipulating a compound microscope. Once these skills are established, students will explore the amazing microscopic world of minerals, humans, single-celled organisms, plants and animals. A variety of mounting techniques will allow the students to examine both living and non-living samples in ethically sensitive ways.

Each section also includes an independent investigation based on the section topic. A number of suggested questions are provided, but the students are encouraged to choose questions of their own and use the microscopes as scientists would. These independent investigations could be the basis for science fair projects.

Notes to the Teacher:

- Plan the activities based on your curriculum requirements. Many substitutions can be made to allow the students to focus on local specimens in order to meet curriculum requirements.

- If you are not familiar with the use and care of compound microscopes, try one before the students begin any of the activities in this book.

- Collect materials well in advance of doing activities and investigations.

- Discuss and practise safety procedures before doing any new activities or using unfamiliar equipment.

Microscopy

- Observe specimens and samples yourself so that you know what the students will be looking at.
- Encourage the students to try other samples of their own choice.
- Time permitting, encourage the students to do the extensions in the activities and investigations as well as in the cross-curricular extensions section. These ideas show how knowledge of the microscopic world can cross subject boundaries.

Objectives

Understanding Basic Concepts

Students will:

- Demonstrate an understanding of the function of the parts of a monocular microscope;
- Describe, using their observations, the characteristics of different types of paper as seen through the microscope;
- Describe, using their observations, the characteristics of different samples of sand as seen through the microscope;
- Describe, using their observations, the characteristics of igneous, sedimentary and metamorphic rocks as seen through the microscope;
- Describe and identify, using their observations, various crystal structures (e.g., salts, sugar, Epsom salt) as seen through the microscope;
- Describe crystal growth as seen through the microscope;
- Describe, using their observations, the various components within a sample of soil (e.g., pebbles, decaying plants) as seen through the microscope;
- Compare different rocks and minerals from the local environment with rocks and minerals from other places;
- Identify and describe, using their observations, the basic structure of animal cells (e.g., human cheek cells, human blood cells, unicellular animals) as seen through the microscope;
- Describe, using their observations, the characteristics of microscopic living things (e.g., yeast, bacteria, unicellular animals) as seen through the microscope;
- Determine the age of a fish based on observations of fish scales as seen through the microscope;
- Observe and describe the structure and function of specialized cells and tissues in different parts of plants (e.g., in roots, stems, leaves);
- Describe, using their observations, differences in structure between plant and animal cells.

Microscopy

Developing Skills of Inquiry, Design, and Communication

Students will:

- Use appropriate vocabulary, including correct science and technology terminology, to communicate ideas, procedures, and results (e.g., use scientific terms such as nucleus, depth of field, xylem);

- Compile qualitative data gathered through investigation in order to record and present results, using diagrams and detailed descriptions;

- Make accurate observations of an object with the naked eye;

- Use a hand lens to make observations of everyday objects;

- Measure the magnifying power of a hand lens;

- Label a diagram of a monocular microscope;

- Learn how to care for a microscope;

- Learn how to bring a specimen into focus using the various objective lenses;

- Learn what depth of field means;

- Observe different planes of focus by 'focusing up and down';

- Describe the advantages and disadvantages of various methods of lighting a specimen;

- Prepare different types of dry mounted (glass slide and tape) and wet mounted (wet and well) specimens (e.g., hair, sand, bacteria, pollen, etc.);

- Design a tool to assist with creating very thin sections of specimens;

- Use stains to increase the visibility of cell structures;

- Discuss the advantages and disadvantages of staining specimens;

- Use a microscope accurately to find, observe, and draw microscopic objects;

- Identify an unknown sample (e.g., sand, hair, spices) based on known samples;

- Compare and describe soil samples from different locations (e.g., different locations in the schoolyard);

- Compare and describe human fingerprint samples;

- Prepare cultures of yeast and bacteria for study; and

- Build a slide trap to hold and observe insects in an ethical manner.

Assessment and Evaluation

Student Effort Rubric   Name: _____

4   I worked on the task with maximum effort.

3   I worked on the task but stopped early.

2   I worked on the task for a while but put very little effort into it.

1   I did not even start the task.

Activity/Investigation																												
Score																												

- -

Student Achievement Rubric   Name: _____

4   I exceeded the objectives of the activity or investigation.

3   I met all of the objectives of the activity or investigation.

2   I met some of the objectives of the activity or investigation but did not meet others.

1   I did not meet the objectives of the activity or investigation.

0   I did not turn in the assignment.

Activity/Investigation																												
Score																												

Assessment and Evaluation

Group Work Rubric

Name: _____

	Possible Points	Points Earned	
		Student	Teacher
The student was prepared for the group work			
The student completed all individual tasks for the group on time			
The student completed all individual tasks for the group correctly and with high quality			
The student participated in the group in a constructive way			
The student shared the responsibility of helping the group get the assignment completed according to the given directions			
Totals			

Additional comments:

_____

_____

- -

Group Work Rubric

Name: _____

	Possible Points	Points Earned	
		Student	Teacher
The student was prepared for the group work			
The student completed all individual tasks for the group on time			
The student completed all individual tasks for the group correctly and with high quality			
The student participated in the group in a constructive way			
The student shared the responsibility of helping the group get the assignment completed according to the given directions			
Totals			

Additional comments:

_____

_____

Assessment and Evaluation

Short Answer Class Checklist
Score each set of short answers on the worksheet pages and track on this page.

Activity/ Investigation #																													
Name Score																													

Assessment and Evaluation

Independent Investigation Rubric

Name: _____

Question

The question is clear and well-focused	4
The question is relatively clear and focused	3
The question is incomplete and unclear	2
There is no question	1
I give myself	
My teacher gives me	

Planning

There was a clear, well-developed plan organized by the student which includes the question, materials, procedure and safety	4
There was a plan, but some assistance from the teacher was required	3
There were steps missing from the plan, teacher organized what the student needed to do	2
There was no plan organized by the student	1
I give myself	
My teacher gives me	

Carrying Out the Investigation

All materials were used safely, appropriately and ethically following learned procedures	4
Most materials were used safely, appropriately and ethically following learned procedures	3
Some materials were used safely, appropriately and ethically and learned procedure is not always followed	2
Materials were not used safely, appropriately or ethically and learned procedures were not followed	1
I give myself	
My teacher gives me	

Reporting

Complete report includes observations and data recorded to clearly answer the question with detail, accuracy and understanding	4
Complete report includes observations and data recorded to answer the question with some detail	3
Incomplete report uses some of the observations and only answers part of the question	2
Incomplete report is missing details and does not answer the question	1
I give myself	
My teacher gives me	

Vocabulary

Arm – attaches the body tube to the base

Base – supports the microscope

Body Tube – tube that supports the eyepiece

Bottom Lighting – lighting that comes from a source under the stage

Coarse Focus Adjustment – knob that controls large adjustments of focus

Compound Microscope – a microscope with multiple lenses, typically one ocular lens in the eyepiece and several other objective lenses in the nosepiece

Cover slip – a thin, square piece of glass used in conjunction with a glass slide. The function of the cover slip is to flatten specimens and also to slow evaporation

Culture – a process used to grow cells

Depth of Field – zone of sharpness; the greater the depth of field, the greater the sharpness of an image

Dermal Tissue – thick-walled cells on the outer part of a plant

Diaphragm – an opening under the stage that can be opened and closed to allow different amounts of light to pass through a specimen

Dry Mounting – a slide preparation technique used with dry specimens and objects

Eyepiece – where you place your eye – a monocular microscope has one of these

Field of View – area of the specimen that can be seen through the microscope with a given objective lens

Fine Focus Adjustment – knob that controls small adjustments of focus

Fixing Slides – a process which preserves and hardens cells or tissues

Fixative – a compound (such as alcohol or formaldehyde) that fixes tissues and cells

Focusing Up and Down – the process of adjusting the fine focus adjustment to bring an object into focus

Ground Tissue – provides storage and support for a plant

Hand Lens – a magnifying device with a single lens

High-Power Objective – a lens with a high power of magnification

Igneous Rock – rock that is formed when molten rock cools and solidifies either below the surface or on the surface

Inclination Point – a point at which the arm can tilt

Lens Paper – a special type of tissue paper that is used to clean the lenses in a microscope

Light Source – a source of light for the microscope; some microscopes use a mirror to reflect light up through the diaphragm

Low-Power Objective – a lens with a low power of magnification

Vocabulary

Magnifying Power – the number of diameters larger an image is than the original specimen; for example, if a lens magnifies an object 5 times, the magnification is said to be 5 diameters, commonly written as "5x"

Metamorphic Rock – rock that is formed when either sedimentary or igneous rock is exposed to extreme temperatures and pressure

Microscope – a magnifier of small objects

Microscopist – a scientist who specializes in research involving microscopes

Microscopy – the study and use of microscopes

Monocular Microscope – a microscope with a single eyepiece/ocular lens; most microscopists prefer binocular microscopes (eyepiece for each eye)

Nosepiece – a rotating device which holds the lenses

Nucleus – a structure (organelle) in cells that contains the DNA and RNA

Ocular Lens – the single lens in the eyepiece of a compound microscope

Osmosis – the movement of liquids through a membrane

Plane of Focus – a point at which the light rays converge, forming a sharp image

Plasma Membrane – a thin structure that completely surrounds the contents of a cell; it controls what goes in and out of the cell

Pollen – fine, dust-like powder that contains the male genetic information from a flower

Saturation Point – the point at which no more solid can dissolve into a liquid

Sedimentary Rock – rock that is formed when small particles of rock settle and eventually harden together

Slide – a thin sheet of glass used to hold objects for examination through a microscope

Specimen – a small piece of tissue, blood, cells, etc. under study

Stage – the flat area on which a slide is placed

Stage Clips – the metal clips which hold a slide to the stage

Stain – to treat specimens with a dye that makes certain structures more visible

Top Lighting – lighting that comes from above the microscope stage

Vascular Tissue – cells responsible for transporting water, sugar and nutrients in a plant

Well Mounting – a variation of the wet mounting technique; in this technique a well is produced in which larger specimens can be held and animals can be free to move around

Wet Mounting – a slide preparation technique used with wet specimens and objects, as well as plants and animals that live in water

Bibliography

Bender, L. (1989). *Atoms and Cells (Through the Microscope Series)*. London: Franklin Watts.

Bender, L. (1989). *Insects (Through the Microscope Series)*. London: Franklin Watts.

Bender, L. (1989). *Plants and Seeds (Through the Microscope Series)*. London: Franklin Watts.

Bender, L. (1990). *Forensic Detection (Through the Microscope Series)*. New York: Gloucester Press.

Kramer, S. (1991). *Hidden Worlds: Looking Through a Scientist's Microscope*. Boston: Houghton Mifflin Co.

Levine, S. (1997). *The Microscope Book*. New York: Sterling Publishing.

Levine, S. (1999). *Fun With Your Microscope*. New York: Sterling Publishing.

Levine, S. (2002). *Science Experiments with a Microscope*. New York: Sterling Publishing.

Nachtigall, W. (1997). *Exploring With the Microscope: A Book of Discovery & Learning*. New York: Sterling Publishing.

Oxlade, C. (1989). *World of the Microscope*. Tulsa, OK: EDC Publishing.

Petersen, C. (2006). *The Microscope: Inventions That Shaped the World*. London: Franklin Watts.

Rainis, K.G. (2005). *Cell and Microbe Science Fair Projects: Using Microscopes, Mold, and More*. Berkeley Heights, NJ: Enslow Publishers Inc.

Rainis, K.G. & Russell, B.J. (1996). *Guide to Microlife*. London: Franklin Watts.

Rogers, K. (2002). *The Usborne Internet-Linked Complete Book of the Microscope*. London: Usborne Books.

Silverstein, A. (1998). *A World in a Drop of Water: Exploring with a Microscope*. Mineola, NY: Dover Publications.

VanCleave, J. (1993). *Janice VanCleave's Microscopes and Magnifying Lenses: Mindboggling Chemistry and Biology Experiments You Can Turn Into Science Fair Projects*. Hoboken, NJ: Jossey-Bass.

Materials

For Viewing

Black construction paper
Goose neck lamp
Hand lenses
Lens tissues
Microscopes – compound
Prepared slides
Small plastic rulers

For Preparing Slides

15 mL measuring spoons
Ballpoint pens
Cover slips
Cutting boards or mats
Distilled water
Eye droppers
Glass slides
Gummed paper or
    self-adhesive plastic
Kettle
Latex gloves
Lab coats
Medicine dropper or eye
    dropper
Methyl or ethyl alcohol
Paper towels
Permanent markers
Pieces of cloth
Plastic cups
Razor blades
Scissors
Slide labels or stickers
Stains
Toothpicks
Transparent tape
Tweezers
Water
White glue

For Collecting Samples

Alcohol wipes
Aquatic nets
Petri dishes
Resealable plastic bags
Sterile lancets

Animal Samples

Dead insects
Fish from fish market
Raw meat

Plant Samples

Carrot roots
Celery stalks
Conifer cones
Cork
Inner skin from an onion
Leaves and leaf stalks
Pollen
Roots
Seeds
Spices
Stems

Other Samples

Alum
Baking soda
Demerara sugar
Dry yeast
Epsom salt
Gravel
Gum eraser
Human hair
Igneous rock
Metamorphic rock
Newspaper
Orange juice
Paper samples
Pebbles
Plain yoghurt
Pony beads
Salad dressing
Sand
Sedimentary rock
Sewing thread
Soil
Sugar cube
Table salt
White sugar

Miscellaneous

Blindfolds
Lined paper
Paper bags
Pencils
Research materials

Look Closely

Skills Activities

Objectives:

1. Make accurate observations of an object with the naked eye.
2. Communicate observations orally.
3. Record observations using diagrams and written descriptions.

Equipment:

Blindfold   Conifer cone   Sugar cube
Leaf   Gum eraser   Cork
Paper bag to put the objects in
Activity 1 Worksheet

Procedure:

1. Work in groups of two or three.

2. Have one group member put on the blindfold then pick one item out of the paper bag.

3. Have that person describe the object out loud based on how it feels. If possible, that person can identify the object.

4. Have that person take off the blindfold and observe with their sense of sight if their identification was correct.

5. Take turns repeating Step 2 with the other group members until all of the objects have been observed.

6. Divide up the objects among the group members. Each person should sketch and write a description of at least two of the objects on their worksheet.

7. Complete the Activity 1 Worksheet.

Name: _____

Look Closely Worksheet

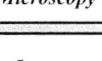

Accurately draw and describe **at least two** of the objects. Use pencil.

Drawing	Drawing	Drawing

Description   Description   Description

_____ _____ _____
_____ _____ _____
_____ _____ _____
_____ _____ _____
_____ _____ _____

?

Discussion:

1. Which descriptive words were based on your sense of touch?

    _____

    _____

2. Which descriptive words were based on your sense of sight?

    _____

    _____

3. Exchange worksheets with the other group members. What other descriptive words did they use?

    _____

    _____

Skills Activities

Using a Hand Lens

Name: _____

Objectives:

1. Practise focusing a hand lens.
2. Measure the magnifying power of a hand lens.

Equipment:

Hand lens (good quality ones, preferably glass)
Research materials (books on lenses, access to computers, etc.)
Lined paper
Activity 2 Worksheet

Procedure:

1. Look at the lines on a piece of paper using a hand lens. Are the lines always in focus? Adjust the height of the lens from the paper until the lines are in focus. Is the distance the same for each person? Discuss with a partner.

2. Measure the magnifying power of the lens using the following method.

   a) Lay the hand lens on the lined paper and count the number of lines from one edge of the lens to the other.
   b) Raise the lens until the lines are in focus. Hold the lens at this height and count the number of lines from one edge of the lens to the other.
   c) Compare the number of lines in step a) with the number of lines in step b).

3. Complete the Activity 2 Worksheet.

Extensions:

1. Measure the magnifying power of different hand lenses.

2. Observe and draw the cross-section shape of a hand lens. Is it flat or curved?

3. Using the internet, find a definition of magnifying power. Explain what magnifying power means to someone else using your own words.

4. Observe the paper through two hand lenses held one on top of the other. What would you say the magnifying power of two lenses is?

Name: _____

Using a Hand Lens Worksheet

Accurately draw the number of lines you see …

Drawing

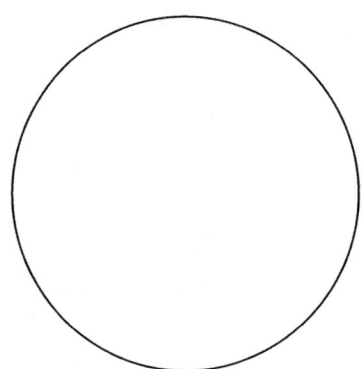

… when the lens is flat on the paper.

Drawing

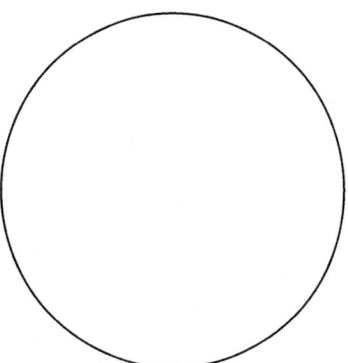

… when the lines on the paper are in focus.

?

Discussion:

1. What would you say is the magnifying power of the lens? Why?

   _____

   _____

2. Research hand lenses and how they work. Write a description below.

   _____

   _____

3. What types of things would not be good to observe using a hand lens? Why?

   _____

   _____

4. What are some of the advantages and disadvantages of using a hand lens instead of the naked eye?

   _____

   _____

Making and Recording Observations

Name: _____

Objectives:

1. Use a hand lens to closely observe objects.
2. Sketch objects while using a hand lens.
3. Begin a list of descriptive words to refer to in the future.
4. Record qualitative and quantative observations of objects.

Equipment:

Hand lens	Small plastic ruler
Activity 3 Worksheet	Activity 3 Word Bank Worksheet
Pencil	

Two mall objects (e.g., seeds, leaves, dead insects, pebbles, etc.)

Procedure:

1. Work in groups of three or four. Make sure each person chooses two objects that the other group members **are not** observing.

2. Carefully observe your two objects using the hand lens. Make accurate drawings of each of the objects on the Activity 3 Worksheet using a **pencil**.

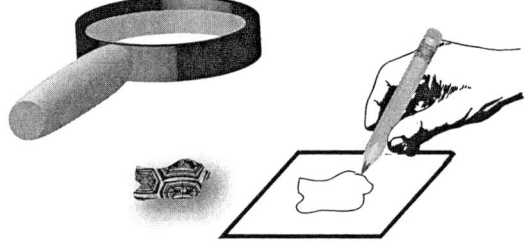

3. Write **at least five** descriptive words for each of the objects in the space below the drawings. Write these descriptive words in the appropriate columns on the Word Bank Worksheet.

4. Put the ruler beside the object and measure the object's length and width and record the measurements on the Activity 3 Worksheet.

Skills Activities

Name: _____

Procedure:

5. Mix up the objects used by the group and place them in the center of the table. Pass your worksheet to another group member. Based on the drawings, description and measurement, find the two objects described on the worksheet. Add that person's descriptive words to your Word Bank Worksheet.

6. Repeat Step 5 with the other members of the group.

7. Answer the questions at the bottom of the Activity 3 Worksheet.

Extensions:

1. Observe other types of objects using a hand lens and describe them.

   Object:

   _____

   _____

   Object:

   _____

   _____

   Object:

   _____

   _____

   Object:

   _____

   _____

2. What types of scientists regularly use hand lenses?

   _____

3. What is another name for a hand lens?

   _____

3

Making and Recording Observations Worksheet

Name: _____

Accurately draw what you see through the lens. Use pencil.

Drawing

Drawing

Description:

_____

_____

_____

Description:

_____

_____

_____

Length: _____

Width: _____

Length: _____

Width: _____

Answers the questions below after switching your worksheets with other group members:

1. Which information most helped you to identify an object? The drawing, the description, or the measurements? Why do you think this is?

_____

_____

2. Which object was the most difficult to identify? Why do you think this is?

_____

_____

3. What other information do you think would be useful to record when making observations of an object?

_____

_____

Name: _____

Making Observations Word Bank

Record descriptive words used to describe objects in the chart below.

Color	
Shape	
Size	
Texture	
Patterning	
Movement	

Microscope Anatomy

Name: _____

Objectives:

1. Name the parts of a compound microscope.
2. Describe the function of the parts of a compound microscope.
3. Label a diagram of a compound microscope.

Equipment:

Compound microscope
Microscope Anatomy Worksheet

Procedure:

1. Look carefully at your microscope and find each of the parts labeled on the diagram below.

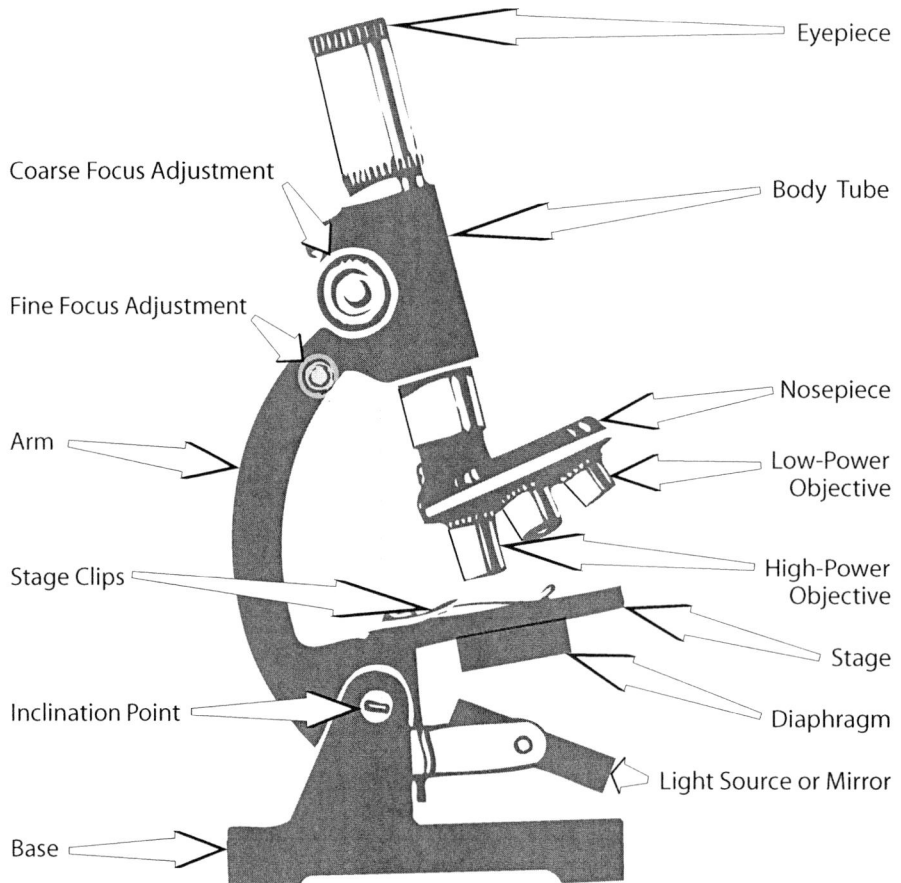

Eyepiece

Coarse Focus Adjustment

Body Tube

Fine Focus Adjustment

Nosepiece

Arm

Low-Power Objective

Stage Clips

High-Power Objective

Stage

Inclination Point

Diaphragm

Light Source or Mirror

Base

2. On the Microscope Anatomy Worksheet, label the parts of the microscope and answer the questions.

Name: _____

Microscope Anatomy Worksheet

Label the parts of the microscope. Use the words below as a reminder.

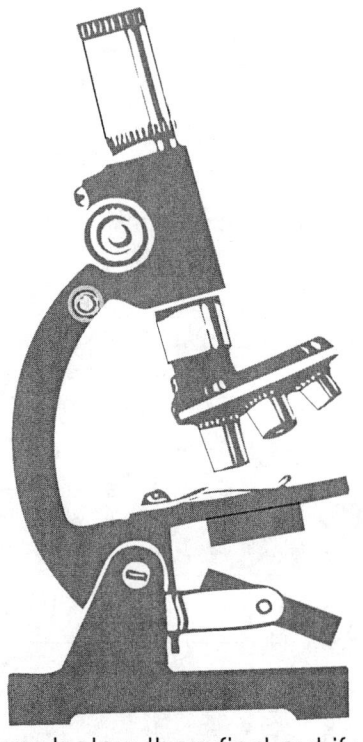

Arm

Base

Body Tube

Coarse Focus Adjustment

Diaphragm

Eyepiece

Fine Focus Adjustment

High-Power Objective

Inclination Point

Low-Power Objective

Light Source (or Mirror)

Nosepiece

Stage

Stage Clips

Answer the questions below then find out if you are correct by using your microscope, a book, or the Internet.

1. What do you think objectives are? Why do you think that microscopes have objectives?

   _____

2. What do you think the coarse focus and fine focus adjustment knobs do?

   _____

   _____

3. What do you think the diaphragm does? Why do you think that a microscope has a diaphragm?

   _____

4. What goes on the stage? What evidence supports your idea?

   _____

5. Why would this type of microscope need a light source or a mirror?

Caring For Your Microscope

Name: _____

Objectives:

1. Learn how to care for a microscope.
2. Create a lab poster which incorporates the rules for microscope care.

Equipment:

This page and Worksheet 5

Procedure:

1. Read the list of microscope care rules below. Why do you think each rule is important?

2. Order the list of rules below from 1 (most important) to 6 (least important). Be prepared to justify your reasons for the order.

☐ Always use two hands to carry a micrscope – one hand on the arm and one hand under the base.

Why? _____

☐ Use lens paper to clean all lenses before and after using the micrscope. Do not use anything other than lens paper to clean lenses.

Why? _____

☐ Avoid touching lenses with your fingers.

Why? _____

☐ Turn off the light when not using the microscope.

Why? _____

☐ Do not leave slides on the stage after you are finished looking at the specimens.

Why? _____

☐ Put the dust cover on the microscope before you put it away.

Why? _____

Name: _____

Caring For Your Microscope Worksheet

In the space below, create a poster to help yourself remember the rules for microscope care. You must include all of the rules.

6

Skills Activities

Name: _____

Troubleshooting

If you encounter any of these problems, try correcting them yourself before asking the teacher for help.

Problem	Possible Reason	Solution
All you see is a black circle	The microscope is not plugged in	Plug in the microscope
	The light is not turned on or the mirror is facing the wrong way	Turn on the light or adjust the mirror
	The diaphragm is closed	Open the diaphragm
The specimen is very dark	The diaphragm is not open enough	Open the diaphragm more
All you see is a white circle	The specimen may not be centered	Try moving the slide
The specimen is very bright and washed-out looking	The diaphragm is open too much	Close the diaphragm slightly
You can see the specimen on low or medium power, but not on high power	There may be too much light	Adjust the diaphragm
	The specimen may not be centered	Try moving the slide
Small spots – which move when you turn the eyepiece	The eyepiece may be dirty	Clean the lenses with lens paper
Small spots – which move when you move the slide	The slide may be dirty	Clean the slide
Small spots – which are only seen when using a certain objective	The objective lens may be dirty	Clean the objective lens with lens paper

Name: _____

Focusing the Microscope

Objectives:

1. Learn how to bring a specimen into focus using the lowest power objective.

Equipment:

Microscope
Prepared slides (each student could have a different slide)
Observation Sheet 1

Procedure:

1. Put the slide on the stage. For this activity, you will not need to use the stage clips as you will be moving the slide around with your fingers.

2. Adjust the nosepiece so that the lens with the **lowest** magnification is the one pointing down at the stage.

3. Using the **coarse adjustment knob**, lower the lens so that it is in its lowest position (closest to the stage). You will know that it is in this position when the knob cannot turn any more.

4. Look through the eyepiece. Can you see the specimen? If not, you may need to move the slide until the specimen is in view.

5. Look at the specimen and decide if the specimen on the slide is in focus. Specimens in focus are not fuzzy around the edges and can be clearly seen. The specimen will probably not be in focus, so focus adjustment will need to be made.

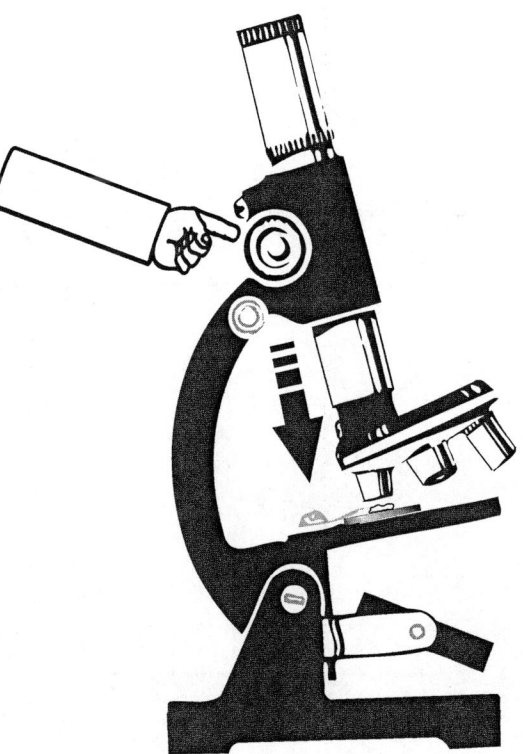

6

Name: _____

Procedure:

6. Slowly turn the coarse adjustment knob in the opposite direction (from when you lowered it). This will raise the lens. The coarse adjustment knob may still not allow you to get a focused image – that is what the fine adjustment knob is for.

7. Slowly turn the fine adjustment knob until the specimen is completely in focus.

8. Complete Observation Sheet 1 for the specimen on your slide.

9. Turn the coarse adjustment knob to raise the lens to the highest position before putting away the microscope.

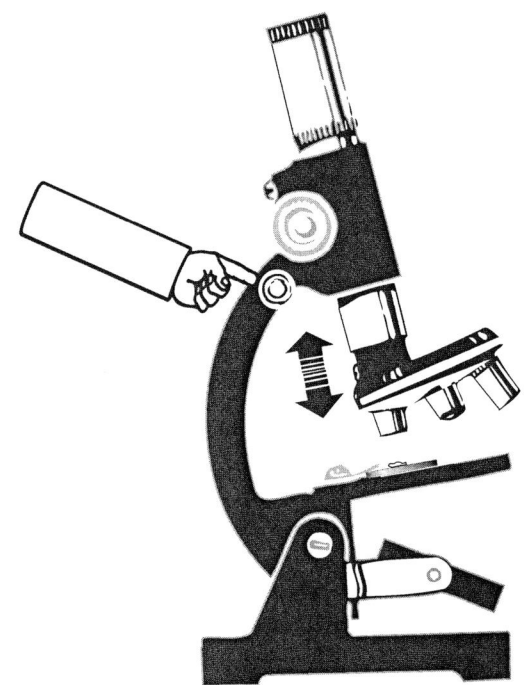

Extensions:

1. Why do microscopes have different adjustment knobs?

   _____

   _____

2. You want to look at another part of the slide, which is to the right. Describe the steps you would take to do this.

   _____

   _____

   _____

   _____

   _____

   _____

Name: _____

Observation Sheet 1

Skills Activities

Date: _____

Specimen: _____

Magnification: _____

Diagram:

Description:

_____

_____

_____

_____

_____

_____

Additional Notes:

_____

_____

_____

_____

_____

_____

_____

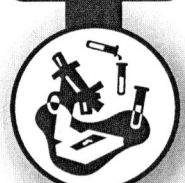

Changing the Lens

Name: _____

Objectives:

1. View a specimen using each of the microscope's objective lenses.
2. Record observations of a single specimen at three different levels of magnification.

Equipment:

Microscope
Prepared slides
Observation Sheet 2

Procedure:

1. Your microscope will have several objective lenses (usually three) with different magnifications. The eyepiece is also a lens and will have its own power of magnification.

2. Find each of the lenses and record their power of magnification in the chart below. The total magnification can be determined by multiplying the magnification of each objective lens with the magnification of the eyepiece (ocular) lens.

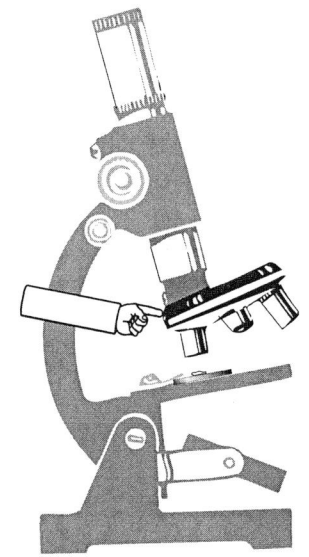

Lens	Objective Lens Magnification	Ocular Lens Magnification	Total Magnification
Low Power			
Medium Power			
High Power			

3. Using the method practised in Activity 6, view your slide using the low power objective lens. Complete the top part of Observation Sheet 2.

Name: _____

Procedure:

4. Rotate the nosepiece so that the medium power objective lens is pointed at the slide and view your slide using the medium power objective lens. Complete the middle part of Observation Sheet 2. Finally, rotate the nosepiece so that the high power objective lens is pointed at the slide and view your slide using the high power objective lens. Complete the bottom part of Observation Sheet 2.

5. What do you notice about the how much of the specimen (field of view) you can see on the different levels of magnification?

    _____

6. When do you think you would use each of the objective lenses? What would be the purpose of each lens?

    _____

    _____

Extensions:

1. Based on your knowledge of the magnification of objective lenses, decide what power you would use to view each of the following: high, medium, or low.

    Grains of salt: _____

    Bacteria: _____

    Insect wings: _____

    Letters on a typewritten page: _____

Observation Sheet 2

Name: _____

Date: _____

Specimen: _____

Diagram:

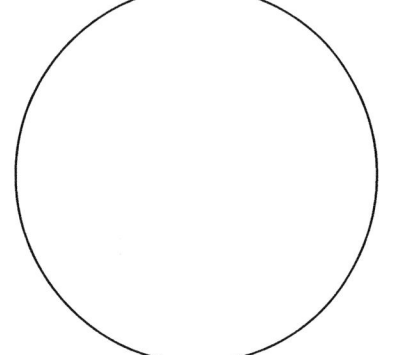

Magnification: _____

Description:

_____

_____

_____

Additional Notes (anything else interesting):

_____

_____

_____

_____

Date: _____

Specimen: _____

Diagram:

Magnification: _____

Description:

_____

_____

_____

Additional Notes (anything else interesting):

_____

_____

_____

_____

Date: _____

Specimen: _____

Diagram:

Magnification: _____

Description:

_____

_____

_____

Additional Notes (anything else interesting):

_____

_____

_____

_____

Skills Activities

Name: _____

Observing Objects in Three Dimensions

Objectives:

1. Observe an object in three dimensions.
2. Observe different planes of focus by 'focusing up and down.'

Equipment:

Microscope   Glass slide
Sewing thread – 3 different colors   Transparent tape

Procedure:

1. Cut a 5 cm piece of thread of each of the three colors.

2. Lay the threads on the glass slide one on top of the other so that they cross in the middle.

   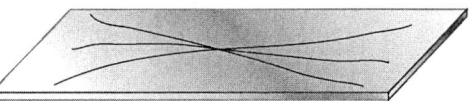

3. Tape the threads to the slide using two pieces of transparent tape.

   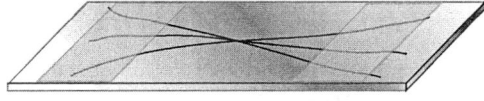

4. Clip the slide to the stage using the stage clips. Move the slide so that the cross of the threads is in the center of the stage.

5. Find the cross of the threads in the field of view using the low power: what do you notice about the other two threads?

   _____

6. Next, focus on the middle thread. What do you notice about the top thread and the bottom thread? Repeat with the bottom thread.

   _____

7. To determine the positions of the three threads, you must slowly raise and lower the objective using the fine adjustment knob. This is know as 'focusing up and down.' Focusing up and down helps us to understand the depth of an object. Why would it be useful for you to know this technique?

   _____
   _____

Using Top and Bottom Lighting

Name: _____

Objectives:

1. Describe how the position of the light source affects observations.
2. Observe a specimen using light from above and light from below.
3. Discuss the advantages and disadvantages of each lighting method.

Equipment:

Microscope   Glass slide
Goose neck lamp   Observation Sheet 2
Piece of gravel or other small opaque object

Procedure:

1. Place the gravel on the slide and center the slide on the stage. Clip the stage clips to the slide.

2. Using the microscope's light or mirror, observe the gravel using low power. This is called bottom lighting. Record your observations on Observation Sheet 2.

3. Turn off the microscope's light. Plug in the goose neck lamp and turn it on so that its light shines on the stage. This is called top lighting. Observe the gravel using low power and record your observations on Observation Sheet 2.

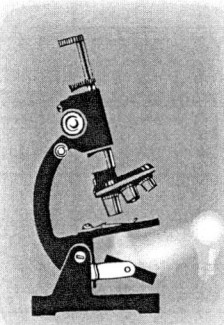

4. How do the different ways of lighting the gravel change the way the gravel looks?

_____

_____

5. When would you use bottom lighting? Why?

_____

_____

Skills Activities

Name: _____

Procedure:

6. When would you use top lighting? Why?

   _____

   _____

7. What are the advantages and disadvantages of each of these types of lighting?

   _____

   _____

Extensions:

1. Observe other objects using both bottom and top lighting. What do you observe?

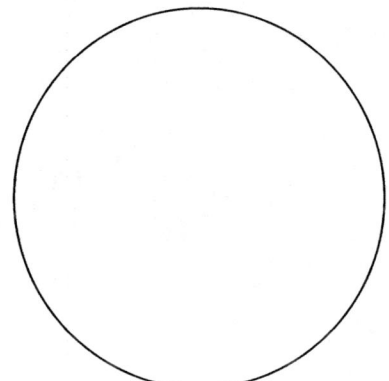

Specimen: _____

Magnification: _____

Description:

_____

_____

_____

_____

_____

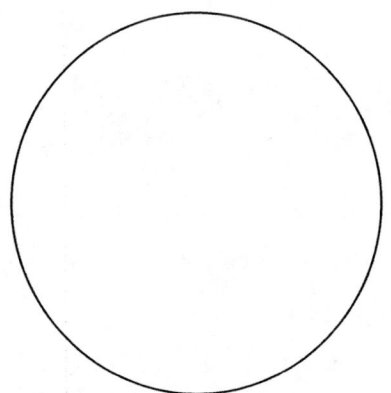

Specimen: _____

Magnification: _____

Description:

_____

_____

_____

_____

_____

Handling Small Objects

Name: _____

Objectives:

1. Use tweezers to lift, move and place small objects.
2. Place small objects on a target.

Equipment:

Microscope   Glass slides (2-3)
Transparent tape   Tweezers
Plastic ruler   Ballpoint pen
White glue   Toothpick
Very small objects (e.g., plant seeds, small gravel, pony beads, etc.)

Procedure:

1. Create the target by placing a piece of transparent tape on the center of a glass slide.

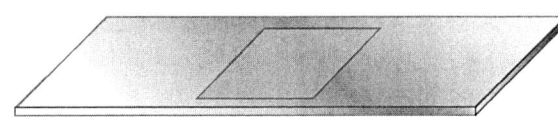

2. Using the ballpoint pen and ruler, draw a cross through the center of the tape. Make it as precise as possible.

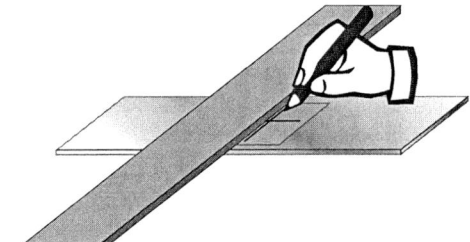

3. Place a small drop of white glue at the center of the cross using a toothpick. You will need to do the next step before the glue dries.

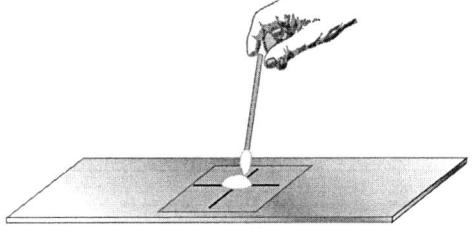

4. Using the tweezers, pick up one of the small objects and place it on the glue. If you drop the object before you get to the slide, try again.

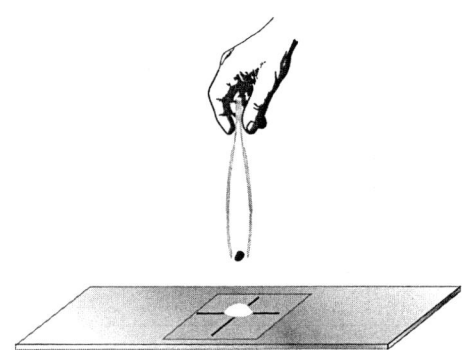

Name: _____

Procedure:

5. Allow the glue to dry slightly and then look at your prepared slide using the low and medium power objective lenses. How close did you come to placing your object on the center of the cross?

6. Repeat steps 1 to 5 with a different type of small object.

7. Which small object was the most difficult to handle? Why?

   _____

   _____

8. Why would the ability to handle small objects be important to a microscopist?

   _____

   _____

9. What tips would you give to someone handling small objects?

   _____

   _____

   _____

Extension:

What else might you use other than tweezers to transfer small objects?

_____

_____

_____

_____

_____

Skills Activities

11a

Skills Activities

Dry Mounting Method 1

Name: _____

Objectives:

1. Prepare a dry mount slide of a specimen.
3. Make a dry mount slide for a class set of slides.
4. Evaluate a partner's dry mount slide.

Equipment:

Glass slide   Cover slip
Scissors   Tweezers
Gummed paper (or self-adhesive plastic)
Fine point permanent marker
Specimens (e.g., plant seed, small leaf, wing from a dead fly, etc.)

Procedure:

1. Place the specimen in the center of the glass slide.

2. Press the cover slip over the specimen.

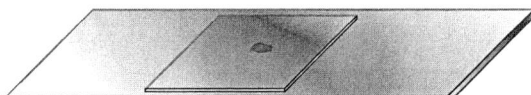

3. Cut a rectangle of gummed paper that is 25 mm x 50 mm.

4. Make a small round hole in the center of the gummed paper that is large enough for you to see all of your specimen, but smaller than the cover slip.

5. Attach the paper (if gummed, you will need to lick it; if adhesive, you may need to remove the backing paper) over the cover slip. Center the hole over the specimen (be sure **not to cover any part of the specimen** with the paper).

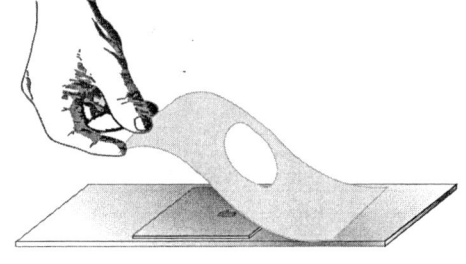

Name: _____

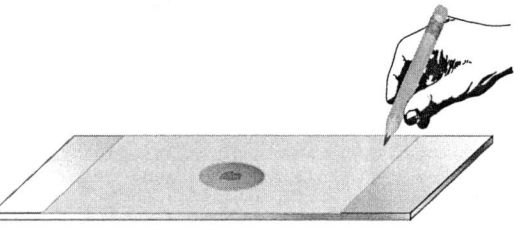

Procedure:

6. Neatly print your name, the type of specimen and the date you made the slide on the gummed paper using permanent marker. The slides will be made into a class set.

7. Look at the slide made by a partner and complete the rating scale below. Be truthful and be prepared to justify your rating.

Your partner's name: _____

Question	0 points for no, 1 point for yes
Is the specimen centered on the slide?	
Was a cover slip used?	
Is the gummed paper 25 mm x 50 mm?	
Is the hole in the center of the paper?	
Is the hole large enough to see the entire specimen?	
Is the entire border of the cover slip covered by paper?	
Is their name, specimen and date printed on the slide?	
Can you easily read their printing?	
Total (out of 8)	

Skills Activities

11a

11b

Dry Mounting Method 2

Name: _____

Objectives:

1. Prepare a dry mount slide using transparent tape.
2. Compare the slide created using this method to the slide made in Activity 11a.
3. Evaluate the advantages and disadvantages of each method of dry mounting.

Equipment:

Microscope   Tweezers
Glass slide   Slide made in Activity 11a
Transparent tape (not translucent type)
Fine point permanent marker
Square white adhesive paper label (such as half of a mailing label)
Specimens (e.g., plant seed, small leaf, wing from a dead fly, etc.)

Procedure:

1. Place the specimen in the center of the glass slide.

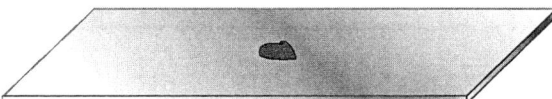

2. Cut a piece of transparent tape that is 50 mm long.

3. Press the tape over the specimen. Try to avoid creating an air bubble under the tape (**hint:** start by pressing down one end of the tape and press towards the other end).

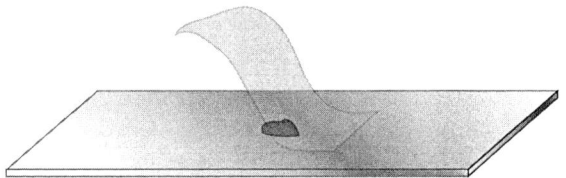

Name: _____

Procedure:

4. Attach the white label to the right of the specimen. Neatly print your name, the type of specimen and the date you made the slide on the label using the permanent marker.

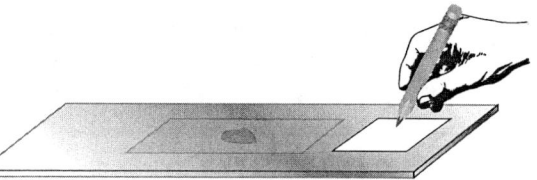
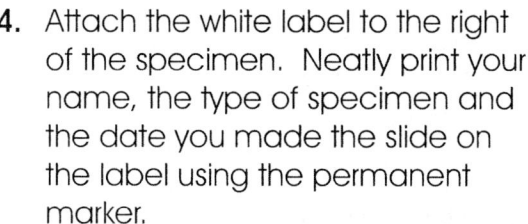

5. Observe the slide made in this activity and the slide made in Activity 11a using low, medium and high power objectives and answer the questions below.

6. What are the advantages and disadvantages of each of these types of dry mounting techniques?

_____

_____

_____

_____

7. Which method of mounting would you use in the future? Why?

_____

_____

_____

_____

Extension:

Can you invent another method for dry mounting a specimen?

_____

_____

_____

_____

_____

Skills Activities

12a

Wet Mounting

Name: _____

Objectives:

1. Prepare a wet mount slide.
2. Create a list of items that would need to be wet mounted.

Equipment:

Microscope	Paper towels
Glass slide	Cover slip
Water	Eye dropper
Observation Sheet 2	Pencil with eraser

Other liquids (e.g., orange juice, salad dressing, etc.)

Procedure:

1. Using the eye dropper, place one drop of water directly in the center of the slide. If you put on too much water, the drop could roll off of the slide and the cover slip may float on top of the water.

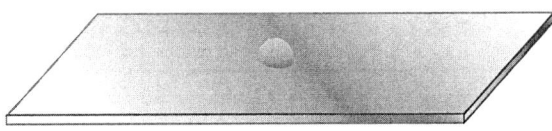

2. Place the cover slip at a 45 degree angle with one edge touching the water drop. Slowly drop the cover slip. If done properly, the cover slip will be flat and centered on the slide and there will be no bubbles visible under the cover slip.

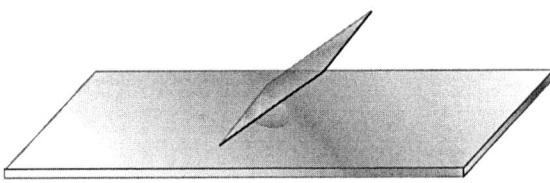

3. Soak up any excess water with a piece of paper towel. Gently press the cover slip down with the eraser end of the pencil to remove any air bubbles.

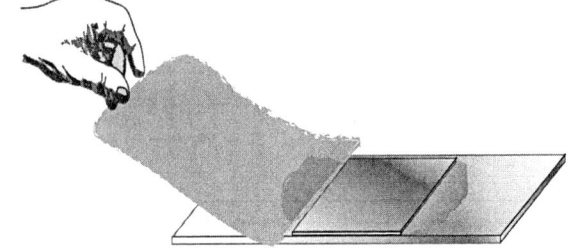

Name: _____

Procedure:

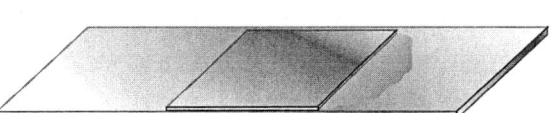

4. Practise making wet mounts using water several more times until you feel that you are confident using the slides, water dropper and cover slips. You can reuse the slide and cover slip by carefully lifting the cover slip and drying both the slide and the cover slip with paper towel.

5. Make a wet mount using one of the other liquids available to you and then observe using low, medium and high power. Record observations on Observation Sheet 2.

6. When do you think that you would make a wet mount? Create a list of things that would need to be wet mounted.

    _____

    _____

    _____

Extension:

Can you think of another method to wet mount a specimen?

_____

_____

_____

_____

_____

Skills Activities

Well Mounting

Objectives:

1. Prepare a well mount slide.
2. Describe when a well mounting technique would be used.

Equipment:

Microscope
Glass slides (2)
Eye dropper
Small metal washer
Petroleum jelly

Water
Cover slips (2)
Ground black pepper
Toothpick

Procedure:

1. Place the metal washer on the center of the slide.

2. Using the eye dropper, place a few drops of water directly in the center of the metal washer. Make sure that the water does not spill over the top of the metal washer. Sprinkle a bit of pepper into the water.

3. Carefully place the cover slip on the metal washer.

4. Practise making a different type of well mount by creating a circle of petroleum jelly with a toothpick on the center of a new slide and then repeat steps 2-4 above.

Name: _____

Procedure:

5. Observe your two well mounts using low, medium and high power objectives.

6. When do you think you would use this well mounting method?

   _____

   _____

   _____

   _____

7. Which method of well mounting (metal washer or petroleum jelly) was most effective? Why do you think this was?

   _____

   _____

   _____

   _____

Extension:

Can you think of another method for well mounting a specimen?

_____

_____

_____

_____

_____

Skills Activities

Making Section Mounts

Skills Activities

Objectives:

1. Cut very thin slides of a specimen.
2. Create a tool to assist with cutting specimens.

Equipment:

Microscope
Cutting board or mat
Plant stem or leaf stalk (e.g., dandelion, parsley, carrot, etc.)

Razor blade
Other materials as required

Procedure:

1. Using the razor blade, cut the thinnest slice of the specimen that you think that you can make. Make sure that you only cut on the cutting board or mat.

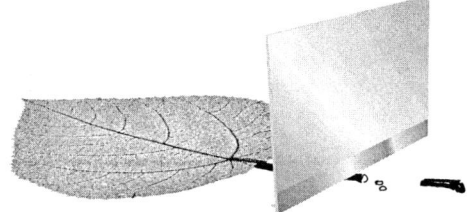

2. In a group of two to three other students, observe each other's slices (also called sections). Determine who has the thinnest section. How could you do this?

_____
_____
_____
_____
_____
_____
_____
_____
_____
_____
_____
_____
_____
_____

Name: _____

Procedure:

3. As a group, think about how you could create a tool to use with the razor blade to make thin, uniform slices. Alternately, your group could research tools which do this. Draw the tool below. You will make this tool after you show your plan to the teacher.

4. Once the teacher accepts your plan, gather the necessary materials and make and try out your tool. Answer the questions below on a separate piece of paper. Your group may submit one set of answers.

a) How does your tool work?

b) What are the advantages of using your tool to cut thin slices versus cutting the slices by hand?

c) What was the greatest challenge in cutting thin slices?

d) On what type of specimens do you think you would use your tool?

e) What safety precautions need to be taken when using your tool?

14

Using Stains

Name: _____

Objectives:

1. Stain a specimen.
2. Discuss the advantages and disadvantages of staining a specimen.

Equipment:

Microscope   Paper towels
Glass slides (2)   Water
Cover slips (2)   Eye dropper
Inner skin from an onion
Latex gloves, lab coats (optional, but recommended)
Stains (e.g., Methylene Blue, Carmine, Iodine, etc.)

Procedure:

1. Using the onion skin, follow the directions for making a wet mount (Activity 12a).

2. Using the eye dropper, place one drop of stain on one edge of the cover slip. Place the flat edge of a piece of paper towel against the opposite edge of the cover slip. The paper will pull the water towards it, and the water will pull the stain under the cover slip.

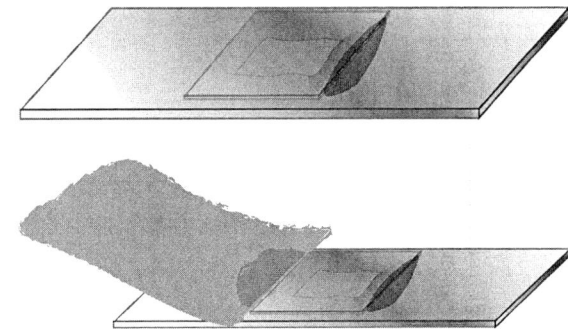

3. As soon as the stain has covered the specimen, you are finished. If the stain does not cover the specimen, use a new piece of paper towel and more stain. Be sure to wipe off any excess stain.

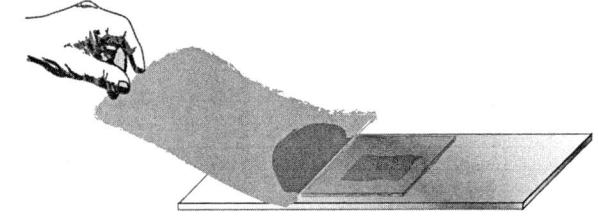

Name: _____

Procedure:

4. Prepare a second wet mounted onion skin **without** stain. Look at both slides using your microscope and answer the questions below.

   Note: **Stain has the name it does for a reason – it stains things!**
   Make sure that the lid of the stain bottle is closed whenever it is not in use.

5. Which stain did you use?

   _____

6. What did the stain do to the onion skin?

   _____

   _____

7. Based on your comparison of the stained and unstained onion skin, what are the advantages and disadvantages of staining a specimen?

   _____

   _____

   _____

Extension:

Survey your classmates to find out which stain they used and their satisfaction with it. Tally your results below. Which stain was most effective?

Stain	Satisfaction Rating (1-10)

Letters Up Close

Investigations

Physical Science

Objectives:

1. Create a dry mount of a letter cut from a newspaper.
2. Observe the orientation and movement of the letter seen through the microscope.

Equipment:

Microscope   Scissors
Glass slide   Cover slip
Gummed paper (or self-adhesive plastic)
Newspaper   Observation Sheet 2

Procedure:

1. Cut an individual letter of the alphabet from the body text of the newspaper.

2. Create a dry mount of the letter using Dry Mount Method 1 (Activity 11a). Position the letter so that it is lined up with the long edge of the slide.

3. Put the slide onto the stage so that the letter could be read normally by you. Before looking through the microscope, predict how the letter will appear under low magnification. _____

4. View the slide using the low power objective lens. Record your observations at the top of Observation Sheet 2. How does this compare to what you predicted? _____

5. When you move the slide to your left across the stage, in which direction does the letter move? What happens when you move it to the right?

   _____

6. When you move the slide away from yourself across the stage, in which direction does the letter move? What happens when you move it towards yourself?

   _____

7. View the slide using the medium power objective lens and the high power objective lens. Record your observations on Observation Sheet 2. What do you notice about the texture of the paper under high power?

   _____

Name: _____

Which Paper is Which?

Objectives:

1. Create a dry mount of a paper sample.
2. Observe the characteristics of different paper using the microscope.
3. Identify a mystery sample of paper.

Equipment:

Microscope   Scissors
Glass slide   Cover slip
Gummed paper   Observation Sheet 3
Permanent marker
Paper sample (e.g., fine paper, paper towel, tissue paper, newsprint, etc.)
Note: the class should prepare samples of 6 different types of paper, and the teacher should prepare a slide of 'Mystery Paper' (one of the six).

Procedure:

1. Cut a 5 mm x 5 mm piece of one of the paper samples and create a dry mount of the paper using Dry Mount Method 1 (Activity 11a). Label the slide with the type of paper that you mounted.

2. Use your microscope to observe slides of the 6 different paper samples created by you and your classmates. Use the same level of magnification to view each. Record observations of each of the types of paper on the top part of Observation Sheet 3. Make a detailed description of each below. You may want to refer to the color and texture words from your Observation Word Bank (Activity 3).

   Sample 1: _____
   Sample 2: _____
   Sample 3: _____
   Sample 4: _____
   Sample 5: _____
   Sample 6: _____

3. When you have completed the sections above, get the slide of the 'Mystery Paper' from your teacher. Observe it using the same level of magnification as the other slides then complete the bottom section of Observation Sheet 3.

Extensions:

1. Add other paper samples.
2. Create your own mystery paper sample for the class.
3. Stain the paper samples and observe. What happens when you stain paper?

Observation
Sheet 3

Name: _____

OTM-270 • SSB1-70 Microscopy

Investigations

Physical Science

Sample 1

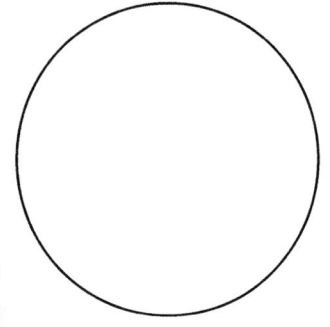

Type: _____

Magnification: _____

Sample 2

Type: _____

Magnification: _____

Sample 3

Type: _____

Magnification: _____

Sample 4

Type: _____

Magnification: _____

Sample 5

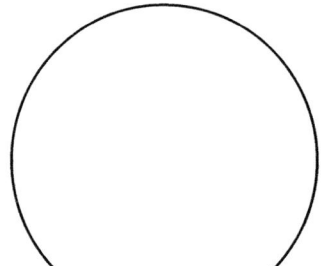

Type: _____

Magnification: _____

Sample 6

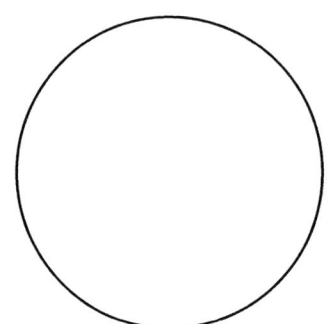

Type: _____

Magnification: _____

Mystery Sample

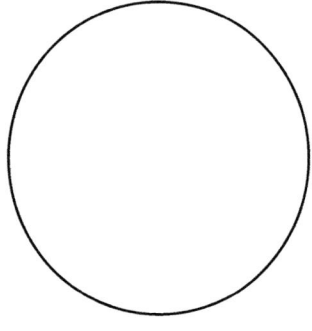

Magnification: _____

I think that the mystery sample is _____

Because:

_____

_____

_____

_____

Name: _____

Sand Mystery

Objectives:

1. Create a dry mounted sample of sand using transparent tape.
2. Observe the characteristics of different sand using the microscope.
3. Identify a mystery sample of sand.

Equipment:

Microscope   Transparent tape
Permanent marker   Observation Sheet 3
Sand sample (Gather different types of sand as a class before the investigation. Note the location of each sample.)
Note: the class should prepare samples of at least 6 different types of sand, and the teacher should prepare a sample of 'Mystery Sand' (one of the six).

Procedure:

1. Based on what you have learned about mounting techniques so far, how would you mount sand?

   _____

   _____

2. What type of lighting would you use when observing sand? Why?

   _____

   _____

3. Cut a 10 cm piece of transparent tape. Fold 2 cm of each of the ends in towards the sticky side. Press a few grains of sand in the center in the sticky part of the tape.

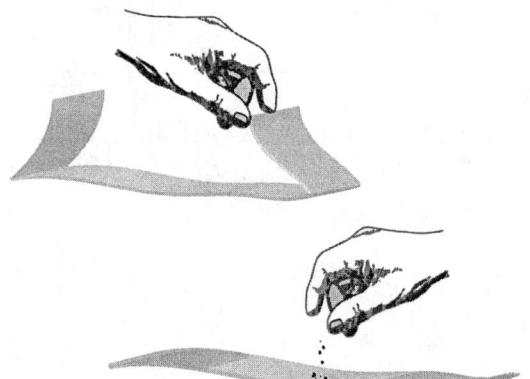

Name: _____

Procedure:

4. Label the tape with the location of the sand that you mounted.

5. Use your microscope to observe samples of the 6 different sand samples created by you and your classmates. Record observations of each of the types of sand on the top part of Observation Sheet 3. Make a detailed description of each below.

Sample 1: _____
_____

Sample 2: _____
_____

Sample 3: _____
_____

Sample 4: _____
_____

Sample 5: _____
_____

Sample 6: _____
_____

6. When you have completed the sections above, get the sample of 'Mystery Sand' from your teacher. Observe it then complete the bottom section of Observation Sheet 3.

Investigations

Physical Science

Name: _____

Rock Classification

Objectives:

1. Observe the characteristics of igneous, sedimentary and metamorphic rocks using the microscope.
2. Record observations of different rock samples.

Equipment:

Microscope   Black construction paper
Goose neck lamp   Observation Sheet 2
Rock samples (at least one type of each: igneous, sedimentary and metamorphic; it is easiest to use a commercial set for this)

Procedure:

1. What type of lighting would you use when observing a rock sample? Why?

   _____

   _____

2. Place the rock on the black construction paper. Center on the stage and top light with the lamp. Observe using low, medium and high power. Record your observations on Observation Sheet 2.

3. What would you say were the distinctive features of each type of rock based on your observations?

   Igneous: _____

   _____

   Sedimentary: _____

   _____

   Metamorphic: _____

   _____

Extensions:

1. Observe other samples of igneous, sedimentary and metamorphic rocks. How do they compare to the rocks you have already observed?
2. Observe fossil specimens in rocks using the microscope. In which type of rock can fossils be found?
3. Observe images of thin sections of rocks on the Internet. How do these images compare with what you observed?

Crystal Shapes

Name: _____

Objectives:

1. Observe different crystal forms.
2. Identify crystals based on their shape.

Equipment:

Microscope   Transparent tape
Permanent marker   Observation Sheet 2
Warm water
Crystal samples (e.g., granules of table salt, white sugar, Epsom salt, alum, Demerara sugar, etc.)
Note: Each person will prepare samples of 3 different types of crystals.

Procedure:

1. Based on what you have learned about sand, how would you mount table salt? _____

2. What type of lighting would you use when observing table salt? Why?

   _____

3. Mount a sample of each of the types of samples. Use your microscope to observe the samples. Record observations of each of the types of crystals on Observation Sheet 3. Identify the shape of each crystal using the diagram to the right.

   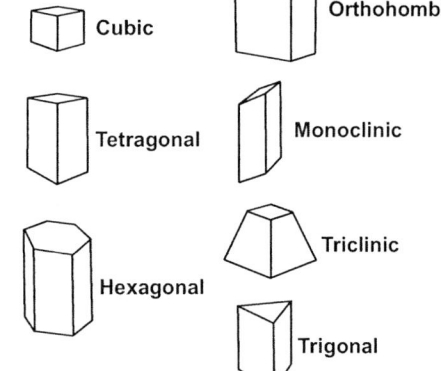

   Sample 1: _____
   Sample 2: _____
   Sample 3: _____

4. Put a few grains of table salt on a glass slide. While observing it with the microscope, add a drop of warm water. What happens?

   _____

Extensions:

1. Create a 'mystery crystal sample' for the class as in Activity 17.
2. Observe a sample of rock salt. How does its crystal structure compare to that of table salt?
3. Find out what alum and Epsom salts are used for.

Investigations

Physical Science

Name: _____

Growing Crystals

Objectives:

1. Observe crystal growth using the microscope.
2. Record observations of crystal structure.

Equipment:

Microscope
Slide label
Clean piece of cloth to cover beaker
Kettle
Observation Sheet 2 (2)
Samples: baking soda, table salt, white sugar and Epsom salt
Glass beakers labelled with the names of the samples (4)

Glass slide
15 mL measuring spoon
Eye dropper

Procedure:

1. You will be working in a group of four. Each group member will prepare a solution of one of the samples in a glass beaker based on the measurements below.

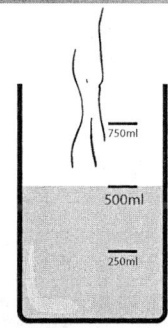

Baking Soda	Table Salt	White Sugar	Epsom Salt
15 mL baking soda	75 mL table salt	180 mL white sugar	75 mL Epsom salt
120 mL hot water	90 mL hot water	75 mL hot water	90 mL hot water

2. **Day 1:** Boil 500 mL water in the kettle. Measure the hot water into the glass beaker. Slowly add the sample a bit at a time while stirring. The solid will dissolve in the liquid until the liquid can hold no more solid. At this point, stirring will not make any more solid dissolve. This is called the *saturation point*.

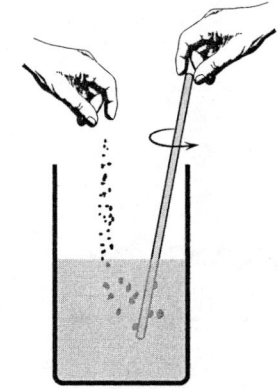

20

Investigations

Physical Science

Procedure:

Day 1 Continued:
Stop at this point, even if you still have solid to add. Put the cloth over the opening and set aside to cool.

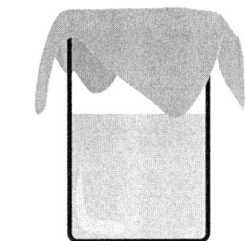

3. **Day 2:** Label a glass slide with the name of your sample. Using the eye dropper, place one drop of your solution on the center of the slide. The heat of the light will begin to make the water evaporate. Record observations on Observation Sheet 2 after 1 minute, 5 minutes and 10 minutes. If the water has not completely evaporated after 10 minutes, make your last observations when it has completely evaporated and make note of the time.

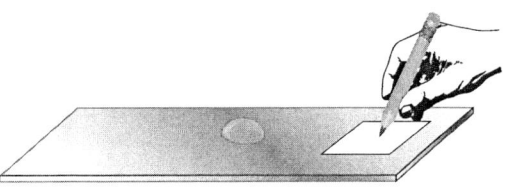

4. Observe the samples made by the other group members. How would you describe each sample? Write a description for each sample on a second copy of Observation Sheet 2.

Extensions:

1. Continue to observe the solutions in the beakers in the days to come by setting them aside in a safe place in the classroom. When all of the water has evaporated, observe the crystals using the microscope. What do you see?

   _____

   _____

2. Why did you need to put the cloth over the beaker?

   _____

   _____

3. Make rock candy by hanging a string in the warm white sugar solution.

   _____

   _____

Name: _____

Soil Sampling

Objectives:

1. Describe the various components within a sample of soil.
2. Compare and describe soil samples from different locations.

Equipment:

Plastic resealable bags   Permanent marker
Microscope   Petri dishes
Observation Sheet 1
Soil sample (gathered in advance)

Procedure:

1. As a class, collect four different soil samples from around the schoolyard or local green space. Keep each sample in a separate plastic bag and label each bag with the location at which the sample was found.

2. You will be working in a group of 4. Each group member will prepare a different soil sample. Each person will look at all four samples.

3. Put a large pinch of the soil sample in the Petri dish. Slide the dish back and forth on a table to allow the materials to spread into a thin layer. This will make the individual soil components easier to see.

4. Using top lighting, observe your soil sample. Make a detailed drawing that includes labels and write a detailed description of the soil components that you see on Observation Sheet 1. If you are unsure what any of the soil components are, check with a classmate or refer to classroom reference books.

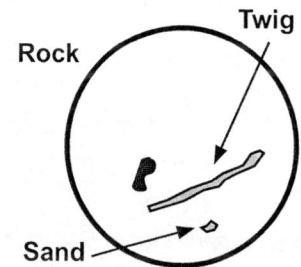

5. Compare your sample to the other three samples in your group and complete the chart below.

Location	How is your sample like this soil sample?	How is your sample different from this soil sample?

Independent Investigations

Physical Science

Objectives:

1. Identify a question about a physical science topic to be independently investigated.
2. Plan and carry out a well-organized independent investigation.
3. Report the findings of an independent investigation.

Procedure:

1. Identify a question about a physical science topic that you would like to investigate. The question should:

   a) Be clear and well-focused.
   b) Require observations through a microscope to answer the question.

2. You may choose a question of your own, or one of the questions below:

   • Do the newspapers in our town use the same type of paper?
   • Which brand of facial tissue has the tightest fibres?
   • Do snowflakes have the same crystal structure as frost?
   • What type of crystals form when salt and sugar are mixed together then dissolved and allowed to crystallize?
   • What is the crystal structure of Acetylsalicylic Acid (ASA)?
   • What are dust bunnies made of?

3. Plan your investigation. You will need to determine which materials you will need, how you will carry out the investigation and the safety considerations that you should keep in mind. You will need to write up your plan and submit it to the teacher **before** you start your investigation.

4. Carry out your investigation. You will need to make sure that you use all materials appropriately, keeping in mind your own safety and the safety of others. Where possible, use the microscope procedures that you have learned. You will need to collect data in the form of written descriptions and drawings that will help you to answer your question.

5. When you have completed your investigation, you will need to create a report (e.g., written, digital, etc.) that includes observations and data recorded during the investigation to clearly answer the question with detail, accuracy and understanding. You may need to do additional research using books and the Internet to help you answer your question.

6. Complete the student portion of the Independent Investigation Rubric.

Name: _____

Making a Cheek Smear

Objectives:

1. Prepare a sample of cheek cells.
2. Observe the basic structure of animal cells.

Equipment:

Microscope   Toothpick (flat type)
Glass slide   Cover slip
Methylene Blue (stain)   Observation Sheet 1

Procedure:

1. Using a toothpick, gently scrape the inside of your cheek. The cells inside your cheeks are called squamous epithelium cells. When you look at the toothpick, you should see a glob of white cells.

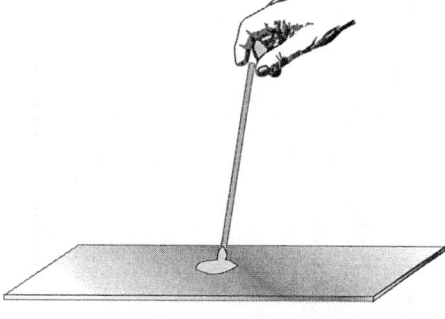

2. Wipe the cells onto the center of the glass slide. Using the edge of a cover slip, scrape the cells (smear) to create the thinnest layer of cells possible. Let the cells air dry.

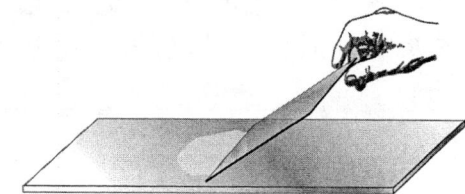

Name: _____

23

Procedure:

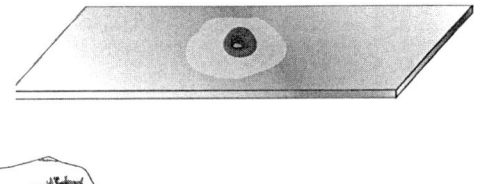

3. Once the smear is dry, add a drop of Methylene Blue stain to the center of the slide and put on the cover slip (review Activity 12a if necessary).

4. First observe the slide at low power to find the cells, then on high power to look at the internal structure of the cells.

5. Create a drawing of what you observe on high power on Observation Sheet 1. You should be able to identify the plasma membrane and the nucleus. The nucleus will appear as a dark circle or oval in the cell. Label the plasma membrane and the nucleus on your drawing.

6. Do you see any of the other internal structures of the cell? What do you think they may be? Use the Internet and other classroom resources to find out.

   _____

   _____

7. Do you see any other types of cells on your slide? If so, what do you think they could be? Use the Internet and other classroom resources to find out.

   _____

   _____

Extensions:

1. Make a cheek smear using different types of stain. Compare these to the cells stained with Methylene Blue.

   _____

   _____

2. Prepare a sample of animal cells from a piece of meat, fish, etc. Compare these to cheek cells.

   _____

   _____

Name: _____

Observing Blood

Objectives:

1. Prepare a sample of blood cells using your own blood.
2. Observe the basic structure of human blood cells.
3. Compare blood cells to cheek cells.

Equipment:

Microscope   Sterile lancet
Alcohol wipes   95% Methyl or ethyl alcohol
Glass slide   Giemsa stain
Eye dropper   Observation Sheet 1
Distilled water in a squeeze bottle   Prepared blood slide (optional)
Note: If you are uncomfortable taking your own blood, use the prepared
blood slide.

Procedure:

1. Wipe your finger with the alcohol wipe. With the sterile lancet, prick your finger. Place a **small** drop of blood off to one side of the slide.

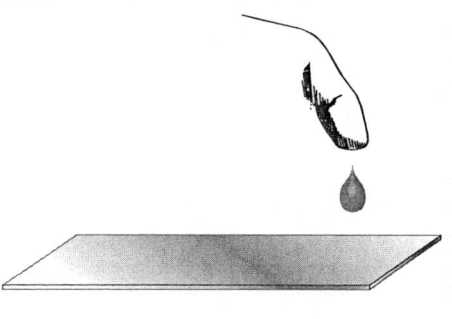

2. Put the cover slip at a 45 degree angle to the slide and touching the blood. Drag the cover slip **away** from the blood drop. This should create a thin layer of blood on the slide.

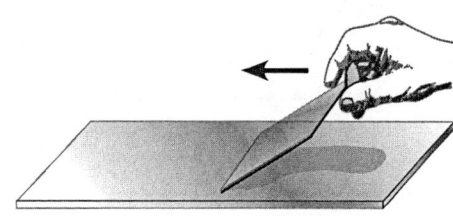

3. Before adding a stain, the cells must be fixed. Fixing the cells allows a stain to be added without damaging the cells due to osmosis. Once the blood smear is dry, add a few drops of Methyl or Ethyl alcohol to the slide using the eye dropper.

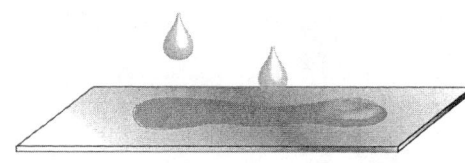

24

Investigations

Human Science

Name: _____

Procedure:

4. Once all of the alcohol has evaporated, add a drop of Giemsa stain. Let the stain air dry on the slide for approximately 15 minutes then rinse gently with room temperature distilled water in a squeeze bottle. Leave to dry. Label with your name and the date.

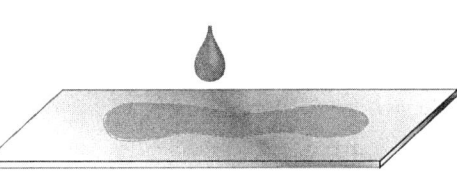

5. First observe the slide at low power to find the cells, then on high power to look at the different types of cells as well as the internal structure of the cells. Record your observations on Observation Sheet 1.

6. What types of cells do you see on your slide? How do you know? Use the Internet and other classroom resources to find out.

   _____

   _____

7. How are the blood cells similar and different than the cheek cells?

   _____

   _____

   _____

Extension:

Research Giemsa stain. Why is it used to stain blood?

   _____

   _____

   _____

   _____

   _____

   _____

   _____

   _____

Name: _____

Comparing Fingerprints

25

Investigations

Objectives:

1. Create transparent tape-mounted fingerprint samples.
2. Look at the similarities and differences between the patterns on your own fingers.

Equipment:

Microscope
Glass slide
HB pencil

Transparent tape 5 to 10 cm
Slide label

Procedure:

1. Using the side of the point of an HB pencil, scribble on a piece of paper.

2. Rub your index finger on the pencil. The graphite will rub off on your finger. Make sure that the entire pad of your finger is covered.

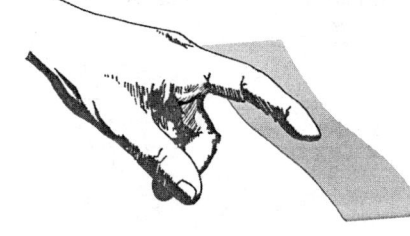

3. Cut a 10 cm piece of transparent tape. Press your graphite-covered finger on the center of the sticky side of the tape. Press the tape on the glass slide. Label the sample with your name and the **finger** and **hand** you made the sample with.

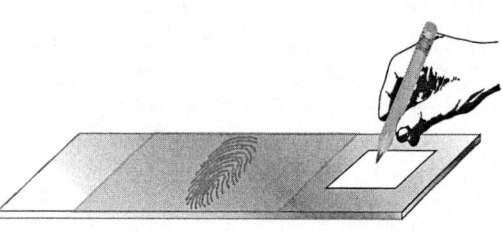

Human Science

Name: _____

25

Investigations

Procedure:

4. Repeat steps 2 and 3 for the remaining fingers and thumb on the same hand. Observe each of the five slides. Draw what you see in the boxes.

Thumb	Index Finger	Middle Finger	Ring Finger	Pinkie Finger

Human Science

5. When you have completed the drawings above, compare the print patterns among your fingers. How are the patterns similar and different?

_____

_____

_____

_____

6. Observe the fingerprints of a classmate. How are his/her fingerprints similar and different to yours?

_____

_____

_____

_____

Extension:

Try the activity again using your other hand. Do the fingerprints on one hand match the corresponding fingerprints on the other?

_____

_____

_____

_____

Name: _____

Hair Mystery

Objectives:

1. Create a dry mounted sample of human hair.
2. Identify a mystery sample of human hair.

Equipment:

Microscope	Glass slide
Cover slip	Permanent marker
Hair sample (your own)	Observation Sheet 3

Procedure:

1. What type of lighting would you use when observing human hair? Why?

2. Collect and mount a strand of your own hair using the dry mounting technique from Activity 11a. The hair should be oriented horizontally. Label the sample with your name.

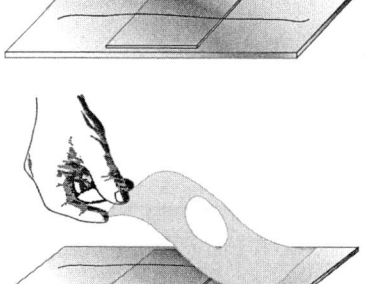
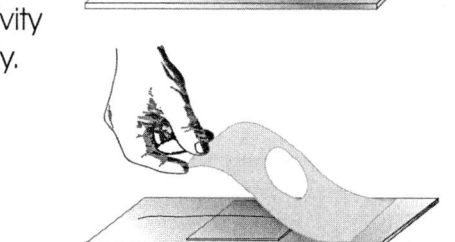

3. Repeat step 2 but do not put your name on this sample.

4. For the next step, you will be working in a group of 6.
   Have the teacher number your unnamed slides from 1 to 6. Your teacher will record whose hair is whose, but will not show you until you get to step 6. Each person should observe each of the six slides and record drawings and observations of the slides on Observation Sheet 3. First find the hair on low power and then make your observations on medium power.

5. When you have completed the top section of the Observation Sheet, observe your own known sample of hair and complete the bottom section of Observation Sheet 3. Which of the unknown hair samples (1-6) was your hair? How did you know? How certain were you that the sample was your own? _____

6. Check with your teacher to find out if you were correct.

27

Human Science

Independent Investigations

Name: _____

Objectives:

1. Identify a question about a human science topic to be independently investigated.
2. Plan and carry out a well-organized independent investigation.
3. Report the findings of an independent investigation.

Procedure:

1. Identify a question about a human science topic that you would like to investigate. The question should:

   a) Be clear and well-focused.
   b) Require observations through a microscope to answer the question.

2. You may choose a question of your own, or one of the questions below:

   • Is it possible to determine if someone's hair has been dyed?
   • Is it possible to determine if someone's hair has been permed?
   • Does all ear wax look the same?
   • Is it possible to determine where on the body a hair comes from?
   • Does a person's fingerprints more closely resemble his/her mother's or father's fingerprints?
   • Does human blood look the same as cow blood?

3. Plan your investigation. You will need to determine which materials you will need, how you will carry out the investigation and the safety considerations that you should keep in mind. You will need to write up your plan and submit it to the teacher **before** you start your investigation.

4. Carry out your investigation. You will need to make sure that you use all materials appropriately, keeping in mind your own safety and the safety of others. Where possible, use the microscope procedures that you have learned. You will need to collect data in the form of written descriptions and drawings that will help you to answer your question.

5. When you have completed your investigation, you will need to create a report (e.g., written, digital, etc.) which includes observations and data recorded during the investigation to clearly answer the question with detail, accuracy and understanding. You may need to do additional research using books and the Internet to help you answer your question.

6. Complete the student portion of the Independent Investigation Rubric.

Name: _____

Growing Yeast

Objectives:

1. Prepare a sample of living yeast.
2. Observe the form of reproduction known as budding.

Equipment:

Microscope   Toothpick (flat type)
Glass slide   Cover slip
Table sugar   Water
Package of dry yeast*   Plastic cup
Iodine (stain)   Observation Sheet 1
*Note: One package of yeast will yield enough samples for an entire class.

Procedure:

1. Mix 30 mL of table sugar into 125 mL of warm water in the plastic cup. Add the package of dry yeast to the water and stir slightly. Let stand at room temperature overnight.

2. What does the yeast look like now? Do you notice anything else?

_____

_____

3. Using a toothpick, take a sample of the yeast. Make a **wet mount** of the yeast sample (review Activity 12a if you need to).

4. Find some yeast cells on low power and then observe again on high power. Find a cell that appears to have bumps bulging out from it. These are called buds and they are new yeast cells that are in the process of breaking free from the parent cell.

5. Draw and describe a budding yeast cell on Observation Sheet 1.

6. **Stain** your sample with iodine (review Activity 14 if you need to). How does using this stain change the appearance of the cells?

_____

Extensions:

1. Find out what yeast is. Is it a plant, an animal or something else?
2. Find out what makes yeast reproduce the most quickly by experimenting with the temperature of the water, the amount of sugar added to the yeast and the temperature at which the yeast spend the night.
3. What is the effect of adding the sugar? Research yeast to find out.

Investigations

Single Cell Science

Examining Bacteria

Name: _____

Objectives:

1. Prepare cultures of bacteria.
2. Examine and identify different types of bacteria.

Equipment:

Microscope
Glass slides
Water
Eye dropper
Plain yoghurt with active cultures

Toothpicks (flat type)
Cover slips
Plastic cups (2)
Observation Sheet 2
Raw meat

Procedure:

1. **Sample 1** – Mix 15 mL of yoghurt into 125 mL of warm water in a cup. Let stand at room temperature overnight. Make a **wet mount** of the yoghurt sample (review Activity 12a if you need to).

2. **Sample 2** – Using a toothpick, remove some of the saliva and plaque from between your teeth. Make a **wet mount** of your saliva sample.

3. **Sample 3** – Place a sample piece (1 cm x 1cm x 1cm cube) of meat in 125 mL of warm water in a cup. Let stand at room temperature for several days. Once the water has become cloudy, remove some of the water using the eye dropper and make a **wet mount** of the meat water sample.

4. For each of the samples, observe the bacteria cells on low power and then observe again on high power. Record what you observe in each of the three samples on Observation Sheet 2.

5. Use the **Key to Bacteria Shapes** on the next page to try to identify the various types of bacteria that you see.

Name: _____

Extensions:

1. Examine prepared slides of bacteria under the microscope and try to find each of the three major types.

2. Try different ways of growing bacteria, such as by touching a piece of potato with your hands or rubbing a cut piece of potato on the floor and then leaving it out for a few days.

3. Find out which type of stain is most effective with bacteria.

4. *Escherichia coli* (*E. coli*) is a type of bacteria found in our digestive tract. *E. coli* from contaminated food can make people very ill. Find out what shape *E. coli* is.

5. Find out what common illness is caused by *Streptococcus* bacteria.

Bacteria come in different shapes...   ...and different arrangements

- sphere = coccus
- spiral = spirillus
- rod = bacillus

- paired = diplo
- clusters = staphylo
- chained = strepto

Key to Bacteria Shapes:

**Bacillus
(rod)**

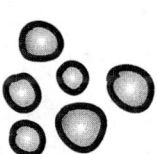

**Coccus
(sphere)**

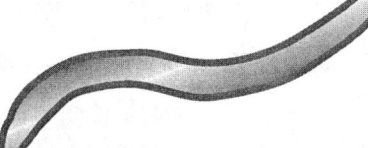

**Spirillum
(spiral)**

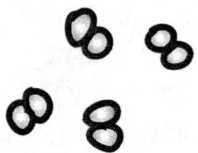

**Diplococcus
(pairs)**

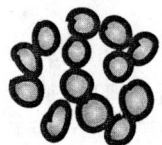

**Staphlococcus
(clusters)**

**Steptococcus
(chains)**

Investigations

Single Cell Science

29

Single-Celled Organisms

Name: _____

Objectives:

1. Identify a question about single-celled organisms to be independently investigated.
2. Plan and carry out a well-organized independent investigation.
3. Report the findings of an independent investigation.

Procedure:

1. Identify a question about single-celled organisms that you would like to investigate. The question should:

   a) Be clear and well-focused.
   b) Require observations through a microscope to answer the question.

2. You may choose a question of your own, or one of the questions below:

   - What happens when yeast is added to grape juice?
   - Is the same type of yeast used to make bread and make beer?
   - Which brand of yoghurt has the most bacteria?
   - What is the effect of bleach on bacteria?
   - How does antibacterial soap work?
   - What is the most effective brand of antibacterial soap?
   - How does ultraviolet light affect the growth of bacteria?
   - Are the cell walls of bacteria affected by temperature.

3. Plan your investigation. You will need to determine which materials you will need, how you will carry out the investigation and the safety considerations that you should keep in mind. You will need to write up your plan and submit it to the teacher **before** you start your investigation.

4. Carry out your investigation. You will need to make sure that you use all materials appropriately, keeping in mind your own safety and the safety of others. Where possible, use the microscope procedures that you have learned. You will need to collect data in the form of written descriptions and drawings that will help you to answer your question.

5. When you have completed your investigation, you will need to create a report (e.g., written, digital, etc.) that includes observations and data recorded during the investigation to clearly answer the question with detail, accuracy and understanding. You may need to do additional research using books and the Internet to help you answer your question.

6. Complete the student portion of the Independent Investigation Rubric.

Observing Microscopic Animals

Objectives:

1. Collect and prepare samples containing microscopic aquatic animals.
2. Examine and identify different types of microscopic aquatic animals.

Equipment:

Microscope   Glass slides
Small metal washer or petroleum jelly   Cover slips
Aquatic net   Plastic jars (2)
Eye dropper   Observation Sheet 2

Procedure:

1. To make an effective collecting net, cut a hole in the end of the aquatic net approximately the same size as the opening of the jar. Tape the jar to the net.

2. Collect a sample from a pond by dragging the net back and forth through the water for at least one minute. Pour the sample into a second plastic jar with a lid.

3. Let the water settle in the jar for several hours before removing a sample. Remove a drop of water from the sludgy part near the bottom of the jar.

4. Prepare a slide for a **well mount** (review Activity 12b if you need to). Place a small drop of the pond water sample in the center of the metal washer or circle of petroleum jelly and carefully put on a cover slip.

5. Observe the slide on low power to look for animals and then observe again on high power. Record what you observe on Observation Sheet 2. Repeat with two other drops of water from the pond water sample. Try to observe as many different types of microscopic animals as possible.

6. Use the **Key to Microscopic Animals** on the next page to try to identify the various types of animals that you saw.

Extensions:

1. Collect samples of water from different ponds, lakes, rivers, etc. Compare the communities of animal life in each.
2. Choose one type of microscopic animal that you have observed and research its lifestyle and habitat.

Investigations

Name: _____

Key to Microscopic Animals:

Mastigophora:

Single-celled animals that move using whip-like body parts called flagella.

Chilomonas   **Chlamydomonas**   **Volvox**   **Pandorina**

         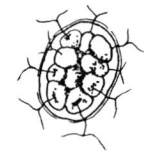

Ciliophora:

Single-celled animals that move using hair-like body parts called cilia.

Paramecium   **Ciliate**   **Vorticella**

Multicellular Animals:

Copopoda   **Daphnia**   **Hydra**   **Ostracod**

   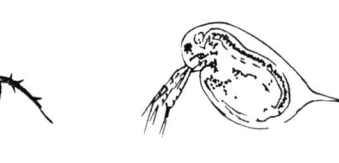      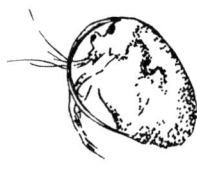

Nematode   **Rotifers**

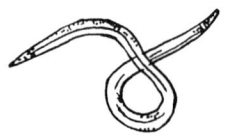   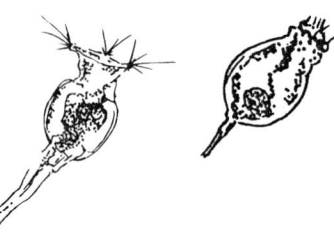

Animal Science

Investigating Insects

Objectives:

1. Examine a live insect specimen in a humane manner.
2. Prepare a slide trap to contain insects while they are viewed.

Equipment:

Microscope
Piece of cardboard
Utility knife
Live insect (small)

Glass slides (2)
Transparent tape
Goose neck lamp
Observation Sheet 1

Procedure:

1. First you will need to prepare a slide trap. To make a slide trap you will need to:

   a) Cut a piece of cardboard the same size as your glass slide.

   b) Cut a slot in the cardboard lengthwise.

   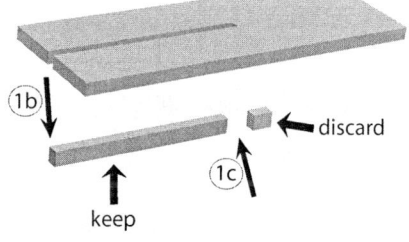

   c) Cut 5 mm off of one end of the cardboard strip that you removed from the large piece of cardboard.

   d) Place the cardboard between two clean glass slides and tape one end.

   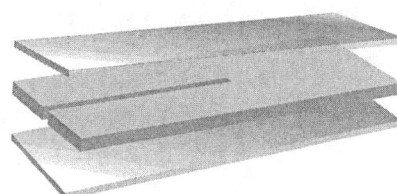

   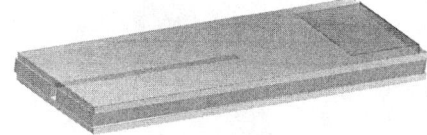

Name: _____

32

Investigations

Procedure:

2. Collect a small live insect, such as an ant, aphid, spider etc.

3. Carefully line up the top slide and put the insect into the slot in the piece of cardboard.

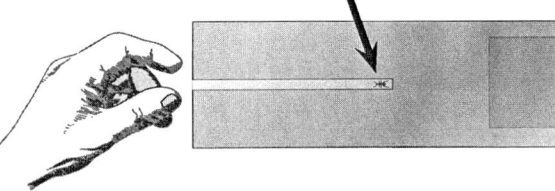

4. Carefully lower the top slide and push the piece of cardboard that you cut out back into the slot to trap the insect.

5. Place the slide on the stage. View the insect with low power and top lighting. Draw a diagram and write a detailed description on Observation Sheet 1. Let the insect go when you are finished observing it.

Extensions:

1. Why would bottom lighting not be appropriate when observing living insects?

2. Describe the challenges you face when observing live animals.

3. Collect and observe other types of small insects.

4. Observe specific insect parts such as butterfly wings, dragonfly wings, etc.

5. Observe dead insects using this method. How are they different from live insects?

6. Design an alternative method for viewing live insects.

Animal Science

Name: _____

Aging Fish

33

Objectives:

1. Prepare wet and dry mounts of a fish scale.
2. Determine the age of a fish based on observations of fish scales.

Equipment:

Microscope   Glass slides (2)
Cover slips (2)   Fish, whole*
Water   Eye dropper
Tweezers   Observation Sheet 1
*Note: One fish will yield enough samples for an entire class.

Procedure:

1. Carefully pull a single scale from the fish using the tweezers. Holding the scale close to its base will help keep it from breaking when you pull it.

2. Mount the scale using a dry mounting technique (review Activity 11a if you need to). Observe the scale using low and then medium power. What do you observe?

   _____

3. You should notice rings that are created as the fish grows. Wide, light-colored bands represent summer growth and narrow, dark-coloured bands represent winter growth.

4. Remove and mount a second fish scale, this time using a **wet mounting** technique (review Activity 12a if you need to). What do you observe this time? Are the bands easier to see when the scale is wet or dry?

   _____

5. What is the age of the fish from which you have taken scales? How did you determine this?

   _____

   _____

6. Make a drawing of a fish scale and add a detailed description on Observation Sheet 1.

Extensions:

1. Observe scales from different parts of the fish.
2. Observe scales from a number of different types of fish. Describe how the scales differ.

Animal Science

Name: _____

Objectives:

1. Identify a question about an animal science topic to be independently investigated.
2. Plan and carry out a well-organized independent investigation.
3. Report the findings of an independent investigation.

Procedure:

1. Identify a question about an animal science topic that you would like to investigate. The question should:

   a) Be clear and well-focused.
   b) Require observations through a microscope to answer the question.

2. You may choose a question of your own, or one of the questions below:

   • Do insects have blood?
   • Why can flies walk up walls?
   • Can you age a butterfly by its scales?
   • How can you tell if a hair comes from a human or a dog?
   • What do animal cells look like when they are growing?

3. Plan your investigation. You will need to determine which materials you will need, how you will carry out the investigation and the safety considerations that you should keep in mind. You will need to write up your plan and submit it to the teacher **before** you start your investigation.

4. Carry out your investigation. You will need to make sure that you use all materials appropriately, keeping in mind your own safety and the safety of others. Where possible, use the microscope procedures that you have learned. You will need to collect data in the form of written descriptions and drawings that will help you to answer your question.

5. When you have completed your investigation, you will need to create a report (e.g., written, digital, etc.) that includes observations and data recorded during the investigation to clearly answer the question with detail, accuracy and understanding. You may need to do additional research using books and the Internet to help you answer your question.

6. Complete the student portion of the Independent Investigation Rubric.

Name: _____

Exploring Celery Cells

Objectives:

1. Observe and identify the major plant tissues in the celery stalk.
2. Prepare a sample of plant cells from a stalk of celery.
3. Observe the basic structure of plant cells.

Equipment:

Microscope
Cover slips
Cutting board or mat
Observation Sheet 2
Razor blade or sectioning tool created in Activity 13

Glass slides
Stalk of celery*
Tweezers

*Note: One stalk of celery will yield enough samples for an entire class.

Procedure:

1. Carefully make a **thin section** of the celery stalk (review Activity 13 if you need to).
2. Mount the celery cross-section using an appropriate mounting technique. Observe the celery cross-section using low power. Record your observations on the top part of Observation Sheet 2.
3. You should see three different types of tissue: dermal tissue, ground tissue and vascular tissue. Use a plant book or the Internet to research what each of these types of tissue looks like and where they are located.
4. Observe the celery at medium power and label the dermal tissue, ground tissue and vascular tissue using the circle in the middle of Observation Sheet 2.
5. Create a drawing of what you observe on high power at the bottom of Observation Sheet 2. You should be able to identify the cell walls and the nucleus of each cell. Label the cell well and the nucleus on your drawing.
6. Compare an animal cell (such as a cheek cell) to a plant cell (such as a cell from the celery). How are they similar and how are they different?

_____

_____

_____

Extensions:

1. Put the stalk of celery in a mixture of food colouring and water for a few days before making a thin section. What does the food colouring do?
2. Research the function of dermal tissue, ground tissue and vascular tissue.

36

Looking at Leaves

Name: _____

Objectives:

1. Prepare a leaf for observation.
2. Observe and identify the major plant tissues in a leaf.

Equipment:

Microscope   Glass slides
Cover slips   Cutting board or mat
Leaves*   Eye dropper
Water   Observation Sheet 2
Razor blade or sectioning tool created in Activity 13
*Note: Each group of three students will look at three different leaves.

Procedure:

1. You will be working in a group of three. Each member of the group will prepare a different type of leaf using the method below.
2. Make sure that your leaf sample is clean and dry. Tightly roll the leaf lengthwise. Carefully make very thin slices off of one end of the leaf using the razor blade. The slices should be so thin that they are almost transparent.
3. You will be looking at the area around the vein, so you may have to cut off the edges of the leaf so that the slice fits under the cover slip.
4. Mount the slice with the inner part of the leaf facing up (so that the inner cells are visible) using an appropriate mounting technique. Observe the leaf cross-section using low power and then medium power.
5. Which of the three types of plant tissue (dermal, ground, vascular) do you see? _____
6. Record observations of your leaf on the top of Observation Sheet 2 and then observe the leaves of your group members and record your observations of their leaves in the middle and on the bottom of Observation Sheet 2.
7. Compare the three leaf cross-sections. How are they similar and how are they different?

_____

Investigations

Plant Science

Extensions:

1. Make and observe cross-sections from other parts of the same leaf.
2. Compare your observations of the celery cross-section to the leaf cross-section.
3. What type of leaf would this method not work well with?

Name: _____

Examining Roots

Objectives:

1. Prepare a sample of plant cells from the root of a carrot.
2. Observe the basic structure of plant cells in a root structure.

Equipment:

Microscope   Glass slides (4)
Cover slips (4)   Carrot root*
Cutting board or mat   Tweezers
Observation Sheet 2
Roots from 3 other plants (e.g., grass, lotus, house plants, etc.)
Razor blade or sectioning tool created in Activity 13
*__Note:__ One carrot will yield enough samples for an entire class.

Procedure:

1. Bring in samples of two different roots of your own choice. They may come from vegetables, house plants, grass from the schoolyard, etc.
2. Carefully make a thin section of the carrot root

3. Mount the root cross-section using an appropriate mounting technique. Observe the root cross-section using low power, medium power and high power.
4. What do you notice about the arrangement of cells in the root cross-section?_____
5. Record your observations of the root at high power on the top of Observation Sheet 2. Label the dermal, ground and vascular tissues on your drawing.
6. Prepare root cross-sections from the other two samples that you brought in. Record observations of each on Observation Sheet 2. How are they similar and how are they different? Why do you think this is?

   _____

   _____

Extensions:

1. Make and observe cross-sections from other root vegetables such as beets and radishes.
2. Compare observations of a carrot with a small diameter to one with a large diameter.

Investigations

Plant Science

Observing Pollen

Name: _____

Objectives:

1. Prepare a sample of pollen from a flower.
2. Observe pollen from a variety of sources.

Equipment:

Microscope   Glass slides
Transparent tape   Slide label
Sources of pollen (e.g., flowers, coniferous trees, etc.)
Observation Sheet 2

Procedure:

1. Bring in a source of pollen. If you are not sure of what pollen is, or where it comes from, research this ahead of time.

2. You will be working in a group of three. Each member of the group will prepare a slide of his/her pollen sample using what he/she thinks is an appropriate method. See Activity 25 for ideas if necessary.

3. Label the sample with the name of the plant that you obtained the pollen from.

4. Find the pollen on low power, then observe the pollen on high power. Create a drawing and write a detailed description of what you observe at the top of Observation Sheet 2.

5. Observe the pollen samples created by the other members in your group. Record observations of each on Observation Sheet 2. How are they similar and how are they different? Why do you think this is?

_____

_____

Extensions:

1. Make and observe pollen from other sources (e.g., other types of flowers, coniferous trees, etc.).
2. How is the pollen from coniferous trees different from the pollen in flowers?
3. What is pollen? Research this to find out.
4. Ragweed pollen gives many people allergic reactions. Find out why the shape of ragweed pollen gives people allergic reactions.

Investigations

Plant Science

Name: _____

Spice Mystery

Objectives:

1. Create a dry mounted sample of a ground spice.
2. Observe the characteristics of different spices using a microscope.
3. Identify a mystery spice sample.

Equipment:

Microscope   Transparent tape
Permanent marker   Observation Sheet 3
Spice, ground (preferably in shakeable spice jars)
Note: The class should prepare samples of at least 6 different types of
spices, and the teacher should prepare a sample of 'Mystery Spice' (one
of the six).

Procedure:

1. Based on what you have learned about mounting techniques, how would
   you mount a ground spice? _____

2. Mount your spice sample using an appropriate mounting technique
   (review Activity 38 if necessary).

3. Use your microscope to observe samples of the 6 different spices created
   by you and your classmates. Record observations of each of the spices
   on the top part of Observation Sheet 3.

4. When you have completed the sections above, get the sample of 'Mystery
   Spice' from your teacher. Observe it then complete the bottom section of
   Observation Sheet 3. What type of spice was the 'Mystery Spice'? How did
   you know?

   _____

   _____

Extensions:

1. What are spices? Where do spices come from?
2. Make your own ground spices by crushing whole spices with a mortar and
   pestle. How do your ground spices compare to the store-bought spices?
3. Find out what each of the spices looks like when whole. Look at the whole
   spices under the microscope.
4. Which spices come from seeds? Which come from other parts of the
   plant?

Investigations

Plant Science

Plant Science

Independent Investigations

Name: _____

Objectives:

1. Identify a question about a plant science topic to be independently investigated.
2. Plan and carry out a well-organized independent investigation.
3. Report the findings of an independent investigation.

Procedure:

1. Identify a question about a plant science topic that you would like to investigate. The question should:

   a) Be clear and well-focused.
   b) Require observations through a microscope to answer the question.

2. You may choose a question of your own, or one of the questions below:

   - Are the cells on the top side of a leaf the same as on the bottom side of a leaf?
   - Do the cells in a living leaf look the same as the cells in a dead leaf?
   - How are stems able to hold a flower up?
   - What gives a flower petal its colour?
   - What is the internal structure of a sesame seed?
   - What types of microscopic plants live in pond water?

3. Plan your investigation. You will need to determine which materials you will need, how you will carry out the investigation and the safety considerations that you should keep in mind. You will need to write up your plan and submit it to the teacher **before** you start your investigation.

4. Carry out your investigation. You will need to make sure that you use all materials appropriately, keeping in mind your own safety and the safety of others. Where possible, use the microscope procedures that you have learned. You will need to collect data in the form of written descriptions and drawings that will help you to answer your question.

5. When you have completed your investigation, you will need to create a report (e.g., written, digital, etc.) which includes observations and data recorded during the investigation to clearly answer the question with detail, accuracy and understanding. You may need to do additional research using books and the Internet to help you answer your question.

6. Complete the student portion of the Independent Investigation Rubric.

Cross-Curricular Extensions

Activity 2:
- Calculate the magnifying power of three stacked hand lenses. (*Mathematics*)
- Find out who first created a hand lens or magnifying glass. What was the reason behind the invention? (*History*)

Activity 3:
- Create a poem about an object using descriptive words from the word bank. (*Language*)
- Create a new category of descriptive words for the Word Bank. (*Language*)

Activity 4:
- Create a mnemonic device to help remember the parts of a microscope. (*Language*)

Activity 7:
- What is 1 mm in micrometers (μm)? When it would be worth measuring in micrometers? (*Mathematics*)
- How much less of the specimen is seen when using each objective lens? (*Mathematics*)

Activity 8:
- Create an art work to be viewed through the microscope that has interesting elements at different planes of focus. (*The Arts*)

Activity 9:
- Create side-by-side color paintings of the same object when viewed using top and bottom lighting. (*The Arts*)

Activity 11b:
- Press flowers or leaves in the pages of a book. Observe through a microscope then put between sheets of adhesive plastic to make bookmarks. (*The Arts*)

Activity 13:
- Write a list of safety rules for using razor blades. (*Language*)
- Calculate the diameter, in micrometers, of the thinnest section made. (*Mathematics*)

Activity 14:
- Research where various stains come from. (*Language*)
- Write a list of safety rules for using stains. (*Language*)

Activity 15:
- Create a secret message for someone that appears in the correct orientation when viewed through the microscope. (*Language*)

Activity 16:
- Research and write an explanatory paragraph about how different types of paper are made and their composition. (*Language*)

Cross-Curricular Extensions

Activity 17:
- Research what types of rock can be found in sand. (*Language*)
- Find out which types of scientists study sand as part of their work. (*Social Studies*)
- Make a microscope picture using grains of different coloured sand. (*The Arts*)

Activity 18:
- Find out which types of scientists study rocks as part of their work. (*Social Studies*)
- Make a textured painting that resembles one of the rocks observed. (*The Arts*)

Activity 19:
- Find out which types of scientists study crystal shapes as part of their work. (*Social Studies*)
- Put in order according to size – table salt, white sugar, Demerara sugar, alum and Epsom salt. (*Mathematics*)

Activity 20:
- Add food colouring to make coloured crystals. (*The Arts*)

Activity 21:
- Measure the various components in a sample of soil in μm. (*Mathematics*)
- Find out which types of scientists study soil as part of their work. (*Social Studies*)

Activity 23:
- Measure the size of a nucleus in a cheek cell in μm. (*Mathematics*)

Activity 24:
- Research and write an explanatory paragraph about a blood disorder. (*Language*)
- How large is a red blood cell in μm? (*Mathematics*)
- Find out which types of scientists study blood as part of their work. (*Social Studies*)

Activity 25:
- Research and write an explanatory paragraph about modern fingerprint analysis techniques. (*Language*)
- Find out when fingerprints were first used in criminology. Who is the person who first used this technique? (*History*)

Activity 26:
- Research and write an explanatory paragraph about modern hair analysis techniques. (*Language*)
- What is the diameter of a human hair? (*Mathematics*)
- Find out which types of scientists study hair samples as part of their work. (*Social Studies*)

Activity 28:
- Find out which types of scientists study yeast as part of their work. (*Social Studies*)
- What is the role of yeast in wine and beer making? (*Social Studies*)

Cross-Curricular Extensions

Activity 29:
- Research and write an explanatory paragraph about E. coli, where it is found in humans and the illnesses it can cause. *(Language)*
- What size are different types of bacteria? *(Mathematics)*
- Find out which types of scientists study bacteria as part of their work. *(Social Studies)*

Activity 31:
- What size are different types of microscopic animals? *(Mathematics)*
- How could you determine the total number of microscopic animals in a drop of water? *(Mathematics)*
- Why are microscopic animals important to fisheries? *(Social Studies)*

Activity 32:
- Write a code of ethics for observing live specimens. *(Language)*
- Put in order according to size – flea, aphid, spider mite and fruit fly. *(Mathematics)*

Activity 33:
- Which industries would need to age fish? Why do they do it? *(Social Studies)*
- Research and write about superstitions related to fish scales. *(Language)*
- Create a painting of a fish scale as seen through the microscope. *(The Arts)*

Activity 36:
- Find out which types of scientists study leaves as part of their work. *(Social Studies)*

Activity 37:
- Make cross-section prints using carrots and beets. *(The Arts)*

Activity 38:
- Research and write a descriptive paragraph about the role that pollen play on a farm. *(Language)*
- Arrange samples of pollen by color. *(The Arts)*
- Find out which types of scientists study pollen as part of their work. *(Social Studies)*

Activity 37:
- Find out where different types of spices are grown. *(Social Studies)*
- Find out which spices originate in North America and which are imported from elsewhere. *(Social Studies)*

Microscope Word and Function Mix & Match

Cut out each of the words and functions. Match each word with the function that describes it.

Hint: the vocabulary list would be a good place to check to find out if a function describes a word.

Arm	Body Tube
Coarse Focus Adjustment	Fine Focus Adjustment
Diaphragm	Eyepiece
High-Power Objective	Low-Power Objective
Inclination Joint	Mirror or Light Source
Base	Nosepiece
Stage	Stage Clips

Microscope Word and Function Mix & Match

Attaches the body tube to the base	Tube that supports the eyepiece
Knob that controls large adjustments of focus	Knob that controls small adjustments of focus
Opening under the stage that can be opened and closed to allow different amounts of light to pass through a specimen	Where you place your eye – a monocular microscope has one of these
Lens with a high power of magnification	Lens with a low power of magnification
A point at which the arm can tilt	A source of light for the microscope
Supports the microscope	A rotating device which holds the lenses
The flat area on which a slide is placed	Metal clips which hold a slide to the stage

Name: _____

Microscopy Crossword

Down:

1. This knob controls large adjustments of focus.
2. This piece supports the microscope.
3. These pieces hold the slide to the stage.
4. This is the piece of the microscope that you look through.

Across:

1. This piece attaches the body tube to the base.
2. This is a sample of tissue or cells.
3. This is the place where slides are clipped.
4. This can bounce light upward through the diaphragm.
5. This tube supports the eyepiece.
6. This device can be opened and closed to let in different amounts of light.
7. This is the name for the lens in the eyepiece.
8. This glass object is a magnifying device.
9. This thin piece of glass goes on the stage.
10. This device holds the objective lenses.

Answer Key

Possible Responses for Activities and Investigations

Activity 2 Worksheet: *(page 19)*

2. The function of a hand lens is to bend light rays to make things look bigger than they are. A hand lens, or magnifying glass, is a bi-convex lens (a lens which is convex on both sides). When an object is closer than the focal point of the lens, the light rays are refracted (bent) inwards and the image appears right-side up and larger than the object. This image is a virtual image, as it does not really exist.

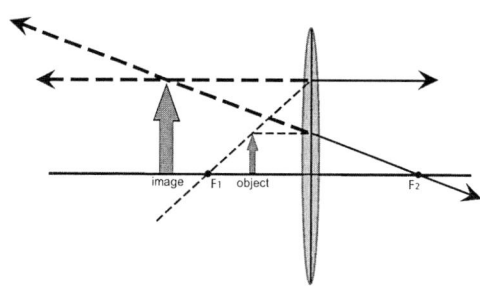

3. Very small objects would require a microscope, rather than a hand lens.

4. The advantage of a hand lens is that small details, not normally visible to the naked eye, are visible. The disadvantage is that a hand lens must be available (the naked eye is always available) and the lens must be of a good quality or the image could be distorted.

Activity 4 Worksheet: *(page 25)*

1. Objectives are the lenses in a microscope. Objective lenses magnify small objects to make them easier to see.

2. The coarse focus knob controls large changes in focus by moving the body up and down. The coarse focus knob is used to help find the specimen. The fine focus knob controls small changes in focus and is used to fine tune the focus once the specimen has been found.

3. The diaphragm is an opening under the stage which can be opened and closed to allow different amounts of light to pass through a specimen. Specimens will be difficult to see if there is too much light or not enough light.

4. The specimen, typically on a glass slide, goes on the stage. The stage is directly above the diaphragm and directly below the body where the lenses are.

5. This type of microscope is used to look through objects. The light travels from the light (or mirror), through the specimen and then up through the microscope to the eye.

Activity 5 Worksheet: *(page 26)*

2. Order of importance may vary. If the microscope is not carried properly, it can be dropped and may be permanently damaged.
   Paper, such as facial tissues, can scratch the surface of the lens.
   Fingers can leave oil on the lens.
   If the light is left on, the bulb can become very hot and burn out.
   Slides left on the stage may fall and break when the microscope is being carried and could accidentally break if a high power objective lens is lowered onto it.
   The dust cover can prevent dust and dirt from getting into knobs and onto lenses.

Activity 7 Worksheet: *(page 32)*

2.

Lens	Objective Lens Magnification	Ocular Lens Magification	Total Magnification
Low Power	4X	10X	40X
Medium Power	10X	10X	100X
High Power	40X	10X	400X

5. At higher levels of magnification, less of the specimen is visible.
6. The low power objective is often used to find a specimen of interest and to center it on the stage. The medium power objective gives a good, detailed overall view of a specimen. The high power objective is used to look at small details (the parts) rather than the entire specimen (the whole).

Activity 8 Worksheet: *(page 35)*
5. When the top most thread is in focus, the other two threads are not in focus and appear blurry.
6. When the middle thread is in focus, both the top thread and the bottom thread are not in focus and appear blurry.
7. This technique is useful to know as specimens are three-dimensional and often there are details at different levels to observe.

Activity 9 Worksheet: *(page 36)*
4. With bottom lighting, the gravel appears as a dark shape. With top lighting, details of the surface of the gravel can be observed.
5. Bottom lighting is used when we want to observe the internal structure of a specimen or object. These specimens or objects must allow at least some light to pass through them.
6. Top lighting is used when we want to observe the external structure of a specimen or object. This technique is useful for opaque specimens or objects.
7. Bottom lighting would not be useful when trying to look at opaque objects, and top lighting would not be useful when trying to look inside objects.

Activity 10 Worksheet: *(page 39)*
7. Small round objects such as seeds or beads tend to be the most difficult to handle as there are no flat edges for the tweezers to grasp.
8. As microscopes are designed to look at very small things, microscopists need to be able to handle very small things when they prepare slides.
9. When handling small objects, it is a good idea to work on a tray, such as a cafeteria tray or a plastic plate. In that way, if an object is dropped, it cannot roll away. Ideally also have more than one of a given object or specimen in case one is lost when preparing the slide.

Activity 11b Worksheet: *(page 43)*
6. The disadvantage of Method 1 is that it requires handling a cover slip, which is very fragile. Also, in Method 1, the sample may be slightly squashed by the cover slip. The advantage of this method is that cover slips are very clear and easy to see through. The sample is also relatively air tight. The disadvantage of Method 2 is that it required handling a piece of tape which can stick to itself and not go where it is supposed to. Also, in Method 2, the sample will get stuck to the tape and air bubbles may be visible. Transparent tape is also typically not as transparent as glass. The advantage of this method is that it is quick and the materials are less fragile.

Activity 12a Worksheet: *(page 45)*
6. Items that require wet mounting would be those that are liquids (e.g., juice and salad dressing, blood, saliva, etc.), specimens that can change when they dry out and microscopic animals and plants that live in water.

Activity 12b Worksheet: *(page 47)*
6. This mounting method can be used to hold larger specimens and in the deeper water animals can be move around freely.

Activity 13 Worksheet: *(page 48)*
2. The thickness of the section could be determined by measuring with a ruler or viewing with a microscope. In the thinnest section, fewer layers of cells will be visible.

Activity 14 Worksheet: *(page 51)*
6. Stains can make certain parts of a specimen more visible.
7. The advantage of staining a specimen is that it can make certain parts of the specimen more visible. The disadvantage is that the stain will change the color of the specimen, so true colors are not viewed. Also, stains can be messy to work with.

Activity 15 Worksheet: *(page 52)*
5. When the slide is moved to the right, the image appears to move to the left. When the slide is moved to the left, the image appears to move to the right.
6. The slide is moved away from the viewer, the image appears to move toward the viewer. When the slide is moved towards the viewer, the image appears to move away from the viewer.
7. Under high power, the plant fibres of the paper can be observed.

Activity 17 Worksheet: *(page 55)*
1. Sand should be mounted using a dry mounting technique.
2. Sand should be viewed using top lighting because rock is typically opaque.

Activity 19 Worksheet: *(page 58)*
1. Grains of table salt can be mounted in the same way as sand using a dry mounting technique.
2. Bottom or top lighting could be used when viewing table salt.
4. The crystals of salt dissolve and seem to disappear in the water.

Activity 23 Worksheet: *(page 64)*
7. At high power, bacteria can sometimes be seen with the cheek cells.

Activity 24 Worksheet: *(page 66)*
6. Red blood cells should be visible. White blood cells may also be visible.
7. Red blood cells are a type of animal cell. Like other animal cells, blood cells have plasma membranes, but fully-matured red blood cells do not have nuclei (plural of nucleus). Red blood cells have a regular, round shape whereas cheek cells have an irregular shape.

Activity 26 Worksheet: *(page 69)*
1. Hair should be viewed using bottom lighting in order to view its internal structure.

Activity 28 Worksheet: *(page 71)*
2. After sitting out overnight, the cup should be full of brown bubbles of yeast. There should also be a distinctive yeast smell, often associated with making yeast bread.
6. Iodine will make the yeast cells appear a deep yellow color.

Activity 33 Worksheet: *(page 79)*
2. Light and dark rings should be visible on the fish scale.
5. Each set of light and dark rings represents one year.

Activity 35 Worksheet: *(page 81)*
6. Both types of cells have plasma membranes, but the plant cell membrane is within a rigid cell wall. Both types of cells have nuclei. In plants, it may also be possible to observe chloroplasts and vacuoles within the cells.

Activity 36 Worksheet: *(page 82)*
5. All three types of tissues (dermal, ground and vascular) should be visible.

Activity 37 Worksheet: *(page 83)*

4. Dermal tissue forms the outer ring, ground tissue lays within that and vascular tissue is found in rays and radiating out.

6. Monocots (plants with single seed leaves and parallel veins) and dicots (plants with paired seed leaves and branching veins) have different arrangements of vascular bundles. In Monocots, the vascular bundles are scattered throughout the ground tissue.

Activity 38 Worksheet: *(page 84)*

5. Pollen from different types of flowers and plants comes in many different shapes and sizes.

Activity 39 Worksheet: *(page 85)*

1. Ground spices can be dry mounted like pollen.

Crossword Puzzle: *(page 92)*

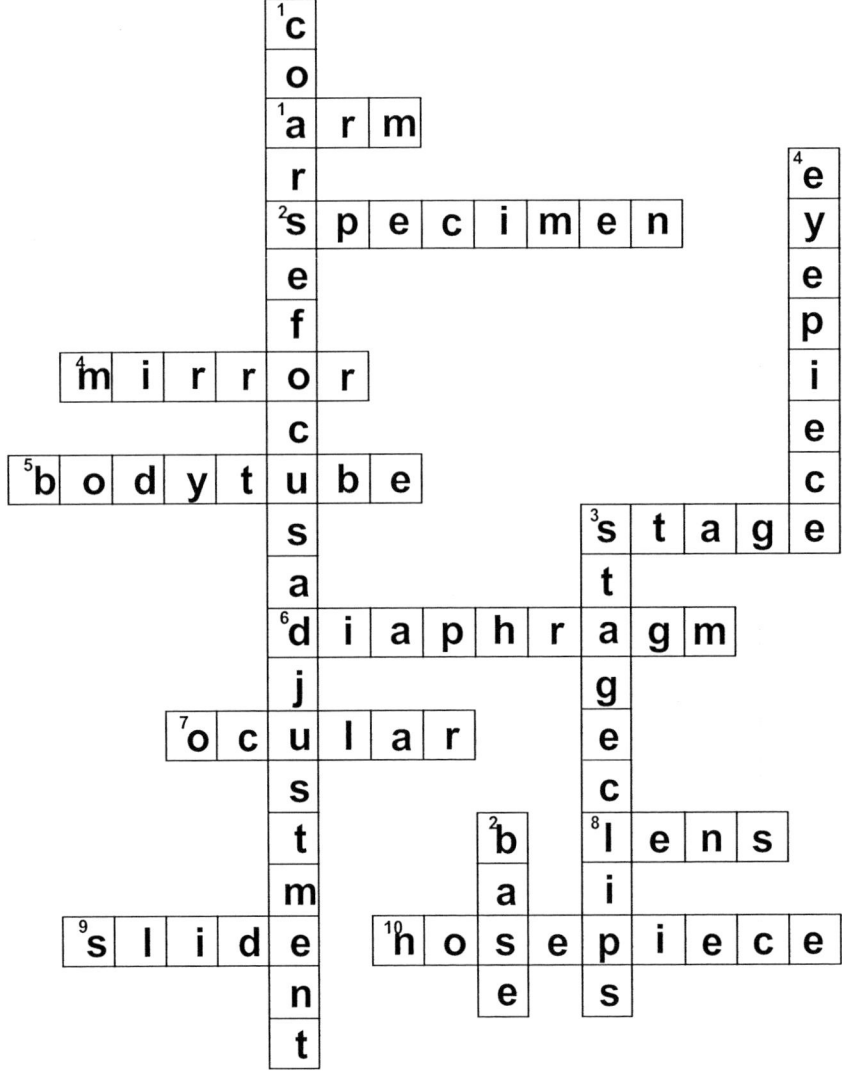

Publication Listing

See Dealer or www.onthemarkpress.com For Pricing 1-800-463-6367

Code #	Title and Grade
OTM-1114	A Graph for all Seasons Gr. 1-3
OTM-1492	Abel's Island LL Gr. 4-6
OTM-2504	Addition Gr. 1-3
OTM-1128	Addition Drills Gr. 1-3
OTM-1131	Addition & Subtraction Drills Gr. 1-3
OTM-14174	Adv. of Huckle Berry Finn LL Gr. 7-8
OTM-267	Al Capone Does My Shirts LL Gr. 4-6
OTM-293	All About Dinosaurs Gr. 2
OTM-102	All About Mexico Gr. 4-6
OTM-120	All About the Ocean Gr. 5-7
OTM-249	All About the Sea Gr. 4-6
OTM-261	All About Weather Gr. 7-8
OTM-2110	All Kinds of Structures Gr. 1
OTM-601	Amazing Aztecs Gr. 4-6
OTM-1468	Amelia Bedelia LL Gr. 1-3
OTM-113	America The Beautiful Gr. 4-6
OTM-1457	Amish Adventure LL Gr. 7-8
OTM-602	Ancient China Gr. 4-6
OTM-618	Ancient Egypt Gr. 4-6
OTM-621	Ancient Greece Gr. 4-6
OTM-619	Ancient Rome Gr. 4-6
OTM-1453	Anne of Green Gables LL Gr. 7-8
OTM-1622	Australia B/W Pictures
OTM-105	Australia Gr. 5-8
OTM-14224	Banner in the Sky LL Gr. 7-8
OTM-401	Be Safe Not Sorry Gr. P-1
OTM-1409	Bear Tales in Literature Gr. 2-4
OTM-14202	Bears in Literature Gr. 1-3
OTM-14257	Because of Winn-Dixie LL Gr. 4-6
OTM-1122	Beginning Math Series: Measurement Gr. 1-3
OTM-1119	Beginning Math Series: Money Gr. 1-3
OTM-1123	Beginning Math Series: Numbers Gr. 1-3
OTM-1108	Beginning Math Series: Shapes Gr. 1-3
OTM-1104	Beginning Math Series: Calendar Gr. 2-3
OTM-1110	Beginning Math Series: Time Gr. 1-3
OTM-1853	Beginning Manuscript D.Gr. PK-2
OTM-1854	Beginning Cursive D. Gr. 2-4
OTM-1857	Beginning and Practice Manuscript D. Gr. PK-2
OTM-1858	Beginning and Practice Cursive D. Gr. 2-4
OTM-1876	Beginning Manuscript Z.B. Gr. PK-2
OTM-1879	Beginning Cursive Z.B. Gr. 2-4
OTM-1882	Beginning and Practice Cursive Z.B. Gr. 2-4
OTM-1883	Beginning and Practice Manuscript Z.B. Gr. PK-2
OTM-14114	Best Christmas Pageant Ever LL Gr. 4-6
OTM-14107	Borrowers, The LL Gr. 4-6
OTM-1463	Bridge to Terabithia LL Gr. 4-6
OTM-2516	BTS La Numeration/Numeration Gr. 1-3
OTM-2517	BTS L'addition/Addition Gr. 1-3
OTM-2518	BTS La Soustraction/ Subtraction Gr. 1-3
OTM-2519	BTS Les Sons/Phonics Gr. 1-3
OTM-2520	BTS La Comprehension de Textes/Reading for Meaning Gr. 1-3
OTM-2521	BTS Les Majuscules et la Ponctuation/ Cap. and Punctuation. Gr. 1-3
OTM-2522	BTS La Redaction de Phrases/ Sentence Writing Gr. 1-3
OTM-2523	BTS La Redaction de Textes/ Story Writing Gr. 1-3
OTM-2524	Numeración Gr. 1-3
OTM-2525	Adición Gr. 1-3
OTM-2526	Sustracción Gr. 1-3
OTM-2527	Fonética Gr. 1-3
OTM-2528	Leer para Entender Gr. 1-3
OTM-2529	Uso de las Mayúsculas y Reglas de Puntuación Gr. 1-3
OTM-2530	Composición de Oraciones Gr. 1-3
OTM-2531	Composici13n de Historias Gr. 1-3
OTM-2513	BTS Handwriting Manuscript D. Gr. 1-3
OTM-2514	BTS Handwriting Cursive D. Gr. 1-3
OTM-2532	BTS Handwriting Manuscript Z.B. Gr. 1-3
OTM-2533	BTS Handwriting Cursive Z.B. Gr. 1-3
OTM-2515	BTS Word Families Gr. 1-3
OTM-14256	Bud, Not Buddy LL Gr. 4-6
OTM-1805	Building Word Families #1 S.V. Gr. 1-2
OTM-1807	Building Word Families #2 L.V. Gr. 1-2
OTM-14164	Call It Courage LL Gr. 7-8
OTM-1467	Call of the Wild LL Gr. 7-8
OTM-2507	Capitalization & Punctuation Gr. 1-3
OTM-14198	Captain Courageous LL Gr. 7-8
OTM-1884	Cartoon Story Starters Gr. 1-3
OTM-1885	Cartoon Story Starters Gr. 4-6
OTM-14154	Castle in the Attic LL Gr. 4-6
OTM-631	Castles & Kings Reading Level 2-4 Gr. 4-6
OTM-1434	Cats in Literature Gr. 3-6
OTM-14212	Cay, The LL Gr. 7-8
OTM-2107	Cells, Tissues & Organs Gr. 7-8
OTM-2101	Characteristics of Flight Gr. 4-6
OTM-1466	Charlie and the Chocolate Factory LL Gr. 4-6
OTM-1423	Charlotte's Web LL Gr. 4-6
OTM-109	China Today Gr. 5-8
OTM-1470	Chocolate Fever LL Gr. 4-6
OTM-14241	Chocolate Touch LL Gr. 4-6
OTM-14104	Classical Poetry Gr. 7-12
OTM-811	Community Helpers Gr. 1-3
OTM-14183	Copper Sunrise NS Gr. 7-8
OTM-1486	Corduroy and Pocket for Corduroy LL Gr. 1-3
OTM-234	Creatures of the Sea Gr. 2-4
OTM-14208	Curse of the Viking Grave LL Gr. 7-8
OTM-1121	Data Management Gr. 4-6
OTM-253	Dealing with Dinosaurs Gr. 4-6
OTM-14105	Dicken's Christmas LL Gr. 7-8
OTM-1621	Dinosaurs B/W Pictures
OTM-216	Dinosaurs Gr. 1
OTM-298	Dinosaurs Gr. 3
OTM-14175	Dinosaurs in Literature Gr. 1-3
OTM-2106	Diversity of Living Things Gr. 4-6
OTM-1127	Division Drills Gr. 4-6
OTM-287	Down by the Sea Gr. 1-3
OTM-1416	Dragons in Literature Gr. 3-6
OTM-2109	Earth's Crust Gr. 6-8
OTM-1612	Egypt B/W Pictures
OTM-14255	Egypt Game LL Gr. 4-6
OTM-628	Egyptians Today and Yesterday Gr. 2-3
OTM-2108	Electricity Gr. 4-6
OTM-285	Energy: The World & You Gr. 4-6
OTM-2123	Environment, The Gr. 4-6
OTM-1812	ESL Teaching Ideas Gr. K-8
OTM-14258	Esperanza Rising NS Gr. 4-6
OTM-1822	Exercises in Grammar Gr. 6
OTM-1823	Exercises in Grammar Gr. 7
OTM-1824	Exercises in Grammar Gr. 8
OTM-1054	Exploring Canada Gr. 1-3
OTM-1056	Exploring Canada Gr. 1-6
OTM-1055	Exploring Canada Gr. 4-6
OTM-820	Exploring My School and Community Gr. 1
OTM-1415	Fables Gr. 4-6
OTM-1639	Fables B/W Pictures
OTM-14210	Fantastic Mr. Fox LL Gr. 4-6
OTM-14168	First 100 Sight Words Gr. 1
OTM-14261	Flat Stanley LL Gr. 1-3
OTM-14170	Flowers for Algernon LL Gr. 7-8
OTM-14128	Fly Away Home LL Gr. 4-6
OTM-405	Food: Fact, Fun & Fiction Gr. 1-3
OTM-406	Food: Nutrition & Invention Gr. 4-6
OTM-2118	Force and Motion Gr. 1-3
OTM-2119	Force and Motion Gr. 4-6
OTM-14263	Fractured Fairy Tales LL Gr. 1-3
OTM-14172	Freckle Juice LL Gr. 1-3
OTM-14260	Frindle LL Gr. 4-6
OTM-1849	Fun with Phonics Gr. 1-3
OTM-14209	Giver, The LL Gr. 7-8
OTM-1490	Great Expectations LL Gr. 7-8
OTM-14169	Great Gilly Hopkins LL Gr. 4-6
OTM-14238	Greek Mythology Gr. 7-8
OTM-2113	Growth and Change in Animals Gr. 2-3
OTM-2114	Growth and Change in Plants Gr. 2-3
OTM-2104	Habitats Gr. 4-6
OTM-14205	Harper Moon LL Gr. 7-8
OTM-14136	Hatchet LL Gr. 7-8
OTM-14184	Hobbit LL Gr. 7-8
OTM-14250	Holes LL Gr. 4-6
OTM-14133	How To Eat Fried Worms LL 4-6
OTM-1848	How To Give a Presentation Gr. 4-6
OTM-14125	How To Teach Writing Through Gr. 7-9
OTM-1810	How To Write a Composition Gr. 6-10
OTM-1809	How To Write a Paragraph Gr. 5-10
OTM-1808	How To Write an Essay Gr. 7-12
OTM-1803	How To Write Poetry and Stories Gr. 4-6
OTM-407	Human Body Gr. 2-4
OTM-402	Human Body Gr. 4-6
OTM-605	In Days of Yore Gr. 4-6
OTM-606	In Pioneer Days Gr. 2-4
OTM-241	Incredible Dinosaurs Gr. P-1
OTM-14177	Incredible Journey LL Gr. 4-6
OTM-14100	Indian in the Cupboard LL Gr. 4-6
OTM-14193	Island of the Blue Dolphins LL 4-6
OTM-1465	James & The Giant Peach LL 4-6
OTM-1625	Japan B/W Pictures
OTM-106	Japan Gr. 5-8
OTM-14264	Journey to the Center of the Earth LL Gr. 7-8
OTM-1461	Julie of the Wolves NS Gr. 7-8
OTM-502	Junior Music for Fall Gr. 4-6
OTM-505	Junior Music for Spring Gr. 4-6
OTM-506	Junior Music Made Easy for Winter Gr. 4-6
OTM-1862	Just for Boys – Reading Composition Gr 3-6
OTM-1863	Just for Boys – Reading Composition Gr. 6-8
OTM-1450	Legends Gr. 4-6
OTM-14130	Life & Adv. of Santa Claus LL 7-8
OTM-210	Life in a Pond Gr. 3-4
OTM-630	Life in the Middle Ages Gr. 7-8
OTM-2103	Light & Sound Gr. 4-6
OTM-14219	Light in the Forest LL Gr. 7-8
OTM-1446	Lion, Witch and the Wardrobe LL Gr. 4-6
OTM-1851	Literature Response Forms Gr. 1-3
OTM-1852	Literature Response Forms Gr. 4-6
OTM-14233	Little House on the Prairie LL 4-6
OTM-14269	Loser LL Gr. 4-6
OTM-14109	Lost in the Barrens LL Gr. 7-8
OTM-278	Magnets Gr. 3-5
OTM-403	Making Sense of Our Senses K-1
OTM-294	Mammals Gr. 1
OTM-295	Mammals Gr. 2
OTM-296	Mammals Gr. 3-4
OTM-297	Mammals Gr. 5-6
OTM-14160	Maniac Magee LL Gr. 4-6
OTM-119	Mapping Activities & Outlines! 4-8
OTM-117	Mapping Skills Gr. 1-3
OTM-107	Mapping Skills Gr. 4-6
OTM-2116	Matter & Materials Gr. 1-3
OTM-2117	Matter & Materials Gr. 4-6
OTM-1116	Measurement Gr. 4-8
OTM-1609	Medieval Life B/W Pictures
OTM-270	Microscopy Gr. 5-8
OTM-1413	Mice in Literature Gr. 3-5
OTM-14180	Midnight Fox LL Gr. 4-6
OTM-14266	Missing May LL Gr. 4-6
OTM-1118	Money Talks Gr. 3-6
OTM-1443	Monkeys in Literature Gr. 2-4
OTM-1497	Mouse & the Motorcycle LL 4-6
OTM-1494	Mr. Poppers Penguins LL Gr. 4-6
OTM-14201	Mrs. Frisby & Rats LL Gr. 4-6
OTM-1826	Multi-Level Spelling USA Gr. 3-6
OTM-1132	Multiplication & Division Drills 4-6
OTM-1130	Multiplication Drills Gr. 4-6
OTM-114	My Country! The USA! Gr. 2-4
OTM-1437	Mystery at Blackrock Island LL 7-8
OTM-14157	Nate the Great and Sticky Case LL Gr. 1-3
OTM-110	New Zealand Gr. 4-8
OTM-1475	Novel Ideas Gr. 4-6
OTM-14244	Number the Stars LL Gr. 4-6
OTM-2503	Numeration Gr. 1-3
OTM-1459	On the Banks of Plum Creek LL Gr. 4-6
OTM-14220	One In the Middle Is Green Kangaroo LL Gr. 1-3
OTM-272	Our Trash Gr. 2-3
OTM-2121	Our Universe Gr. 5-8
OTM-286	Outer Space Gr. 1-2
OTM-118	Outline Maps of the World Gr. 1-8
OTM-1431	Owls in the Family LL Gr. 4-6
OTM-1452	Paperbag Princess LL Gr. 1-3
OTM-212	Passport to Australia Gr. 4-5
OTM-1804	Personal Spelling Dictionary Gr. 2-5
OTM-503	Phantom of the Opera Gr. 6-9
OTM-2506	Phonics Gr. 1-3
OTM-1133	Picture Book Math Gr. 1-3
OTM-1448	Pigs in Literature Gr. 2-4
OTM-1499	Pinballs LL Gr. 4-6
OTM-634	Pirates Gr. 4-6
OTM-2120	Planets Gr. 3-6
OTM-1874	Poetry Prompts Gr. 1-3
OTM-1875	Poetry Prompts Gr. 4-6
OTM-624	Prehistoric Times Gr. 4-6
OTM-1855	Practice Manuscript D. Gr. PK-2
OTM-1856	Practice Cursive D. Gr. 2-4
OTM-1880	Practice Manuscript Z.B. Gr. PK-2
OTM-1881	Practice Cursive Z.B. Gr. 2-4
OTM-501	Primary Music for Fall Gr. 1-3
OTM-504	Primary Music for Spring Gr. 4-6
OTM-507	Primary Music for Winter Gr. 1-3
OTM-14262	Prince Caspian LL Gr. 4-6
OTM-1120	Probability and Inheritance Gr. 7-10
OTM-1426	Rabbits in Literature Gr. 2-4
OTM-1444	Ramona Quimby Age 8 LL 4-6
OTM-2508	Reading for Meaning Gr. 1-3
OTM-1876	Reading Logs Gr. K-1
OTM-1877	Reading Logs Gr. 2-3
OTM-14162	Reading with Arnold Lobel Gr. 2-3
OTM-14234	Reading with Arthur Gr. 1-3
OTM-1440	Reading with Beatrix Potter 2-4
OTM-14129	Reading with Beatrix Potter: Biography Gr. 2-4
OTM-14200	Reading with Curious George Gr. 2-4
OTM-14230	Reading with Eric Carle Gr. 1-3
OTM-14126	Reading with Franklin Gr. 1-3
OTM-14251	Reading with Kenneth Oppel 4-6
OTM-1427	Reading with Mercer Mayer 1-2
OTM-14171	Reading with Phoebe Gilman Gr. 2-3
OTM-14142	Reading with Robert Munsch Gr. 1-3
OTM-14140	Reading with Kids at Bailey Elem. School Gr. 2-4
OTM-14167	Reading with Magic School Bus Gr. 1-3
OTM-14247	Reading with Magic Treehouse Gr. 1-3
OTM-14225	River, The LL Gr. 7-8
OTM-508	Robert Schumann-Life & Times Gr. 6-9
OTM-265	Rocks & Minerals Gr. 4-6
OTM-269	Rocks & Soils Gr. 2-3
OTM-14103	Sadako and 1 000 Paper Cranes LL Gr. 4-6
OTM-404	Safety Gr. 2-4
OTM-1442	Sarah Plain & Tall LL Gr. 4-6
OTM-1601	Sea Creatures B/W Pictures
OTM-279	Sea Creatures Gr. 1-3
OTM-1464	Secret Garden LL Gr. 4-6
OTM-2502	Sentence Writing Gr. 1-3
OTM-1430	Serendipity Series Gr. 3-5
OTM-1866	Shakespeare Shorts – Performing Arts Gr. 2-4
OTM-1867	Shakespeare Shorts – Performing Arts Gr. 4-6
OTM-1868	Shakespeare Shorts – Language Arts Gr. 2-4
OTM-1869	Shakespeare Shorts – Language Arts Gr. 4-6
OTM-14158	Shilo LL Gr. 4-6
OTM-14181	Sight Word Activities Gr. 1
OTM-2100	Simple Machines Gr. 1-3
OTM-299	Simple Machines Gr. 4-6

Code #	Title and Grade	Code #	Title and Grade	Code #	Title and Grade	Code #	Title and Grade
OTM-2122	Solar System Gr. 4-6						
OTM-111	South American Countries Gr. 4-6						
OTM-1644	South American B/W Pictures						
OTM-205	Space Gr. 2-3						
OTM-1814	Spelling Gr. 1						
OTM-1815	Spelling Gr. 2						
OTM-1816	Spelling Gr. 3						
OTM-1817	Spelling Gr. 4						
OTM-1818	Spelling Gr. 5						
OTM-1819	Spelling Gr. 6						
OTM-1834	Spelling Blacklines Gr. 1						
OTM-1835	Spelling Blacklines Gr. 2						
OTM-1836	Spelling Blacklines Gr. 3						
OTM-1837	Spelling Blacklines Gr. 4						
OTM-1827	Spelling Worksavers #1 Gr. 3-5						
OTM-2125	Stable Structures & Mech. Gr. 3						
OTM-14139	Stone Fox LL Gr. 4-6						
OTM-14214	Stone Orchard LL Gr. 7-8						
OTM-1864	Story Starters Gr. 1-3						
OTM-1865	Story Starters Gr. 4-6						
OTM-1873	Story Starters Gr. 1-6						
OTM-2509	Story Writing Gr. 1-3						
OTM-2111	Structures, Mechanisms & Motion Gr. 2						
OTM-14211	Stuart Little LL Gr. 4-6						
OTM-2505	Subtraction Gr. 1-3						
OTM-1129	Subtraction Drills Gr. 1-3						
OTM-2511	Successful Language Practice Gr. 1-3						
OTM-2512	Successful Math Practice Gr. 1-3						
OTM-2309	Summer Learning Gr. K-1						
OTM-2310	Summer Learning Gr. 1-2						
OTM-2311	Summer Learning Gr. 2-3						
OTM-2312	Summer Learning Gr. 3-4						
OTM-2313	Summer Learning Gr. 4-5						
OTM-2314	Summer Learning Gr. 5-6						
OTM-14159	Summer of the Swans LL Gr. 4-6						
OTM-1418	Superfudge LL Gr. 4-6						
OTM-108	Switzerland Gr. 4-6						
OTM-115	Take a Trip to Australia Gr. 2-3						
OTM-2102	Taking Off With Flight Gr. 1-3						
OTM-1455	Tales of the Fourth Grade LL 4-6						
OTM-1135	Teaching Math Through Sports Gr. 5-8						
OTM-1134	Teaching Math with Everyday Manipulatives Gr. 4-6						
OTM-14265	The Breadwinner LL Gr. 4-6						
OTM-14259	The Tale of Despereaux LL Gr. 4-6						
OTM-1472	Ticket to Curlew LL Gr. 4-6						
OTM-14222	To Kill a Mockingbird LL Gr. 7-8						
OTM-14163	Traditional Poetry Gr. 7-10						
OTM-1481	Tuck Everlasting LL Gr. 4-6						
OTM-14126	Turtles in Literature Gr. 1-3						
OTM-14270	Underground to Canada LL Gr. 4-6						
OTM-1427	Unicorns in Literature Gr. 3-5						
OTM-617	Viking Age, The Gr. 4-6						
OTM-14206	War with Grandpa LL Gr. 4-6						
OTM-2124	Water Gr. 2-4						
OTM-260	Weather Gr. 4-6						
OTM-1417	Wee Folk in Literature Gr. 3-5						
OTM-808	What is a Community? Gr. 2-4						
OTM-262	What is the Weather Today? 2-4						
OTM-1473	Where the Red Fern Grows LL Gr. 7-8						
OTM-1487	Where the Wild Things Are LL Gr. 1-3						
OTM-14187	Whipping Boy LL Gr. 4-6						
OTM-14226	Who is Frances Rain? LL Gr. 4-6						
OTM-509	Wolfgang Amadeus Mozart Gr. 6-9						
OTM-14213	Wolf Island LL Gr. 1-3						
OTM-1859	Word Families 2, 3 Letter Words Gr. 1-3						
OTM-1860	Word Families 3, 4 Letter Words Gr. 1-3						
OTM-1861	Word Families 2, 3, 4 Letter Words Big Book Gr. 1-3						
OTM-620	World Explorers Gr. 4-6						
OTM-14221	Wrinkle in Time LL Gr. 7-8						